BRUM AND BRUMMIES

Volume 4

BRUM AND BRUMMIES

Volume 4

Carl Chinn

BREWIN BOOKS

First published in 2005 by
Brewin Books, Studley, Warwickshire B80 7LG
www.brewinbooks.com

British Library Cataloguing in Publication Data
A catalogue record for this book is available from
The British Library

ISBN: 1 85858 236 9

Typeset in Times
printed in Great Britain by Warwick Printing Company Limited,
Theatre Street, Warwick, Warwickshire CV34 4DR.

Contents

To all Brummies
proud of our city and
proud of our forebears

Chapter 1:
Brummies

From Blitz to VE Day

D Day, 6 June 1944, was a momentous event that heralded the liberation of western Europe from the cruelty of Nazism. As the biggest sea-borne invasion in history, however, it presented massive logistical problems. Five infantry divisions – two British, two American and one Canadian – had to be shipped from England to the coast of France. These divisions included about 133,000 men – in addition to which a further 23,500 airborne troops were parachuted behind enemy lines to secure strategic targets.

Protected by the Royal Naval and other Allied naval bombardments, tens upon tens of thousands of men had to clamber down into landing craft to be taken under fire to the beachheads and then wade through the water to gain land. As they did so, tanks and a variety of vehicles were driven out of the sea to support them, whilst over 11,000 Allied aircraft cleared the skies of the Luftwaffe. Under attack from the Germans and with the high sea at their back, the troops had to secure their positions quickly and move inland as fast as possible to ensure the success of the landings. They did so, although some major targets such as Caen were not taken as quickly as had been hoped.

In the first three weeks of Operation Neptune, the assault phase of the Allied Invasion of Europe, the mighty total of almost 7,000 ships and landing craft transported nearly 200,000 vehicles and 600,000 tons of supplies. These vehicles were essential to the thrust forward of the Allied armies, but they could only move if they were supplied with the vital resource of oil. Fuelled up before they left England, the tanks and vehicles had to be refuelled regularly and that was accomplished by PLUTO – the Pipe Line Under The Ocean. The designated petrol terminal for this pipeline was Port-en-Bassin, the place where the United States and British Forces met, between Omaha and Gold Beaches. This was ten miles away from Arromanches – the small port and spa town that was taken early on during D Day by the British 50th Division. Number 47 (Royal Marine) Commando was given the task of capturing Port-en-Bassin. They did their job swiftly and effectively on the same day.

A fuel terminal was then established which could supply all the Allied forces. At first an armoured pipeline was laid under the sea to receive fuel from tankers offshore, but soon a pipeline was laid that crossed under the breadth of the English Channel from the Isle of Wight to a place near to the Normandy port of Cherbourg. Eventually four PLUTO pipelines were in operation and remained so until French ports were cleared and made safe for Allied shipping. These pipelines supplied 2,500 tons of petrol each day to allow the Allies to push ahead. It is impossible to conceive a situation whereby the Battle of Normandy could have been won without PLUTO and its oil – and that is where a Birmingham firm, British Timken Limited of Cheston Road, Aston played a crucial role. Manufacturers of ball and roller bearings, this firm made the actual bearings for PLUTO. Its factory was one of the first hit in Britain, back on 26 August 1940 when the Battle of Britain was still raging, and its workers highlighted the importance of Birmingham to the British war effort.

But Birmingham's contribution to the munitions industry was even vaster. The fact that the Luftwaffe was unable to knock out the Royal Air Force in the Battle of Britain owed much to the workers of the Spitfire factory in Castle Bromwich, Birmingham. By the end of the war, they were producing 320 Spitfires and 20 Lancasters a month - more aircraft than any other factory in the UK. Elsewhere in the city at Longbridge, men and women turned out 2,866 Fairey Battles, Hurricanes, Stirlings and Lancasters; whilst at the nearby Austin works almost 500 army and other vehicles were made each week - as well as a multitude of other goods.

Indeed, the array of war work in Birmingham was staggering. Bristol Hercules engines made at Rover; Lancaster wings, shell cases and bombs manufactured at Fisher and Ludlow's; Spitfire wing spans and light alloy tubing at Reynold's; and plastic components at the GEC. Up to the Battle of Britain all the aero-carburettors for the RAF's Spitfires and Hurricanes were made at SU Carburettors - and if it had been destroyed the air force would have suffered a mortal blow. Serck produced all the radiators and air coolers for these planes. Workers at the Dunlop, Kynoch's, the Norton, James Cycle, Lucas, the Metropolitan-Cammell, Morris Commercial, the Wolsley, and the BSA (Birmingham Small Arms) all strove hard for victory. Indeed, when the BSA was hit badly in November 1940, Churchill himself was alarmed at the consequent national fall in the making of rifles.

Smaller and medium-sized firms were also crucial with their wares, from the clothing fasteners of Newey Brothers to the blow lamps of Samuel Heath's. Turner Brothers made a wide range of jigs and tools critical for aircraft production; Eddystone Radio and the Monitor Radio Company were significant in their field; jewellers turned their hands to intricate parts; and Hudson's Whistles supplied whistles to the Royal Navy and others. By 1944, 400,000 Brummies were involved in war work - making up a greater percentage of the population than any other place in the United Kingdom. Whenever we rightly honour and remember the men of the D Day landings and other battles, let us also hold in our minds all the workers that also played their part in the fight for freedom.

Birmingham is the second largest city in the United Kingdom and is renowned as the city of a 1,000 trades. Both its people and industry played a vital role in the British war effort, but that essential contribution is little known outside the city. Birmingham was the second most heavily bombed city in the country, and along with the whole of Merseyside it lost more of its citizens to enemy action than any other place outside London. The Blitz killed 2,241 Brummies and seriously injured another 3,010, with 3,682 harmed slightly. Countless thousands had their minds and souls scarred, and many Brummies live still with the anguish caused by the Blitz on the City.

The Luftwaffe's air raids began on 9 August 1940 and ended on 23 April 1943, although the most destructive air raids occurred between the end of August 1940 and May 1941. Prolonged and powerful attacks destroyed 12,391 houses, 302 factories, 34 churches, halls and cinemas, and 205 other buildings. Thousands of other properties were damaged. This destruction was not immediately noticeable to strangers, scattered as it was throughout central Birmingham - an area with a population equal to that of Bolton or Cardiff. The spread of bomb damage partly accounts for the lack of appreciation of the hardships endured by Brummies - but much of that ignorance is because of government censorship.

Censors sought to stifle knowledge of bombing raids nationally, but with regard to London, Coventry, Portsmouth and elsewhere their efforts quickly broke down. However, in Birmingham's case their work was successful, and in December 1940 the editor of the city's *Evening Mail* explained that 'the experts, time and again have assured us that the publication of detailed particulars regarding air damage would be slipping a useful card into the enemy's hands'. The effectiveness of the censors

Women from Wright's Ropes, Garrison Street, Bordesley, showing their determination to beat Hitler. These women made ropes for ships.

probably resulted from their understanding of Birmingham's importance to the nation's war effort. In a secret paper written before Dunkirk, the Chiefs of Staff had told the Prime Minister, Winston Churchill, that 'Germany could gain complete air superiority unless she could not knock out our air force, and the aircraft industries, some vital portions of which are concentrated at Coventry and Birmingham'. The efforts of the people of Birmingham during the Second World War have often been overlooked, whilst the sacrifice of those who died has been forgotten. Overlooked and forgotten by all bar the people of Birmingham, who remain proud of the city's role in overcoming tyranny.

The end of the war in Europe on 8 May 1945 marked the end of war-time production and the beginning of the hope that Birmingham would rebuild itself. It was all the more poignant because the City had been bombed so heavily and so many lives had been lost. Sixty years and more on, VE Day still has the power to resonate with us. It calls out to us of that huge sigh of relief that swept the land at the news that Germany had surrendered. It calls out to us of the joy that overwhelmed everyone at the knowledge that the war in Europe was over. It calls out to us of the pride that infused each person at the awareness that Britain had stayed free and had defeated the Nazis. And it also calls out to us of the sorrow that so many mothers and fathers, wives and husbands, sons and daughters felt because their loved ones would not join in the great release of emotions because they had paid the ultimate sacrifice with their lives.

It is impossible for those who did not live through the war to embrace all those feelings, but through the words of those who did live through the war, who did endure its hardships and who knew what was at stake then younger generations can make that vital leap of historical imagination to understand more fully what it was like to live in war-time Britain. We must always listen to those who worked and fought for our freedom. Brummies were foremost amongst them, both in the services and in the munitions factories. Those of us of us who did not experience the war can only say in words that could never capture our deepest thoughts – we thank you for your sacrifices; we thank you for patriotism; we thank you for giving your todays for our tomorrows; and we thank you for allowing us to grow up and live in peace and freedom. We shall remember.

Auxiliary Fire Servicemen dowting the fires on the Moseley Road on 26 October 1940. Thanks to the Birmingham Evening Mail. The autumn and winter of 1940 were hard times for Brummies as the Luftwaffe targeted the City's numerous munitions factories. On 24 October the 'city's firefighters were again in great difficulties', as enemy bombers pounded the City. Shortly after midnight 189 major fires were blazing. There were deaths and damage across the city centre. A shelter in Cox Street, Hockley was hit and 25 people were killed. The Empire Theatre was burned out, whilst the Hippodrome was saved from destruction by 'the diligence and courage of a handful of members of the male staff who smothered the incendiary bombs before they could get a hold on the roof'. Next door, Tony's Ballroom 'burned fiercely'. ('Scars of War', Birmingham Mail, 9 December 1940).

Early in the morning of 25 October G.J. Ball caught the 5 a.m. tram to town, on his way to work at the B.S.A. plant in Redditch. Alighting at Martineau Street he walked to New Street. He recalled that 'In the middle of the road where there had been an island was a crater with a gas main still burning fiercely. To the left just inside New Street, Marshall and Snelgrove (posh) shop was wrecked by bombs and twisted black girders were hanging out of the road. I walked through the station to catch a Midland Red bus to Redditch in Bromsgrove Street. Nothing remained of one end of the street, where once had been a kosher butcher and the outfitters Sword and Robb Ltd, were just ruins.'

That evening the Carlton Picture House in Sparkbrook was bombed. The manager had told the customers to sit in the stalls beneath the balcony of the circle. This gave some protection but despite this precaution nineteen people were killed. Most of them were *sitting in the rows nearest to the screen. ('Cinema Bombed', Birmingham Mail, 26 October 1940). There were numerous casualties amongst other Brummies on the night of 25 October and there were many heroes and heroines. One of them was Ivy Gilbert who put out incendiaries which fell in her street, modestly stating 'it was nothing'. Another was Arthur Bryant. He was the nightwatchman at the Lansdowne Laundry in Studley Street, Sparkbrook where there were three shelters. As the raid began he directed about 50 women and children to safety. He was watching the last mother and baby go into a shelter when a fire bomb hit one end of the laundry. The blast threw him down the stairs and 'when I recovered my senses I saw the place was beginning to burn'. He and a friend 'got out most of the people from the shelters, for it was getting too hot for them' and took them to a nearby school. Returning to the laundry the men led out the horses from the stable, even though 'the place was going well now', and Arthur drove three of the firm's vans away from blaze. Then he telephoned the fire service and helped fight the blaze and save the rear of the laundry itself. ('Raid Gallantry', Birmingham Mail, 26 October 1940).*

Barbara Young came across this photograph and thinks that 'apparently it was taken in the back yard where I used to live in Monument Road, Ladywood on V. E. Day. You can just about see the flags at the top of the photograph. I thought you might like this. I know that the lady on the front row is my mother Clarice Turner. On her lap is my sister Margaret and next is my sister Pauline and next but one is me, Barbara. I do not know the names of the other people, but obviously they used to live close by and were celebrating together.'

A few years back, Violet Reynolds kindly handed me a magnificent illuminated address to place in my archive in Birmingham Central Library. The address was presented to Arthur Reynolds, a shopkeeper of 159, Wheeler Street – which lay between Great King Street, Hockley and Clifford Street, Lozells. In this photo Arthur is receiving the address at a special night at the 'Acorn Hotel', which was just up from his shop. A report in a local newspaper explained why Arthur had been so honoured.

It stated that 'throughout the war years one name has been on the lips of residents of Wheeler Street, Lozells, the name of the man who organised everything – Mr Arthur Reynolds. Whether it was the man who organised the children's parties, or the man who brought them a cup of tea and a cigarette after the worst of Birmingham's blitzes, it was still the same – Mr Arthur Reynolds. And last night, at a convivial gathering at the Acorn Hotel, Wheeler Street, once again Mr Reynolds' name was to the fore. But this time the gathering was of a rather different nature – very different indeed from the days when there were scores of people sheltering at the fire watchers' HQ when the Luftwaffe was over-head.

'This time business residents and shopkeepers of Wheeler Street had met in a joint effort to show their appreciation of non-smoker, teetotaller Mr Reynolds' wartime

efforts in the form of a presentation of a gold watch and illuminated address –
especially in recognition of his work as chief of the firewatching service during the
war. The manager of the Acorn Hotel, Mr C Hayes, hit the right note when he said that
many of Wheeler Street's residents owed their lives to Mr Reynolds' activities, to say
nothing of the many long months he spent watching over their business premises;
acting as father of the flock of over 200 people who used to gather nightly in the
nearest air raid shelter, and bringing them cigarettes from his own shop when the
dawn brought realisation of the damage and disaster of the raids.

'Mr Reynolds had little to say in reply to the presentation – obviously emotion was
too strong for him to make an elaborate speech. But, if one could judge by the
applause which greeted his brief remarks, Wheeler Street still recognises that,
whatever the difficulty, there is a friend in need in Mr Reynolds.'

The illuminated address reads: 'Presented by the Business People of Wheeler St.
Lozells, Birmingham to Mr Arthur Reynolds in recognition and appreciation of
services rendered as organizer of the Local Fire Party during the world war 1939-
1945. We desire to express our very best wishes for your future welfare & sincerely
hope that the one above who rules all our destinies will grant you a full share of the
blessings of life which to our opinion you justly deserve. Feb 12th/1946.'

Colourful Characters of Old Brum

Characters abounded in Old Brum. Noisy, colourful, distinctive, charismatic and passionate their kind are few and far between today. We live in a world that is sanitised, homogenised and refined, where anyone out of the ordinary is eschewed and frowned upon. It is a world that does not value those who dare to speak up and to challenge, that shies away from those who are radical, free-thinking, daring and spirited. Unhappily the characters of Brummagem would not find a place in the new Birmingham, especially in the new Bull Ring, with its swanky shops and swish shoppers. They belonged to the Bull Ring of Memory, the Bull Ring that was rough and ready yet always familiar and embracing to working-class Brummies.

Just bring them to mind. Percy Shurmer, the Miskin King, who strove with might and main for the rights of the poor. He and his supporters forced the Council to replace the overflowing miskins of the back-to-back courtyards with proper dustbins and to put in gas stoves in each home; he had his own band; and he collected money form whomsoever he could to pay for parties for parties for his Sparrows, the poor kids of Brum. A councillor and later MP, Shurmer's resolve to do something good for those in need was matched by Ernie McCulloch, the Prince of Beggars. He was another who did whatever he could to raise funds for kids from the back streets, so that he might take them on a day trip to Sutton Park and buy them clothes.

Then there was Jimmy Jesus, supposedly the son of wealthy parents, who called out for all that would listen to help him 'Feed my lambs'; the escapologist, the man in chains, who would have himself tied and wait for his cap to be filled with coppers and silver before he released himself; and, of course, the 'Andy Carrier Lady. Small and with eyes that did not see, she stood on the steps by the old Market Hall, almost chirrupping out, 'andy carriers, andy carriers', and selling her brown paper bags to anyone that would spare a copper or two to buy one.

Her urgings to buy were often overwhelmed by the calls from the barrow boys and market traders, people like Percy Moseley, Winnie Harte, Johnny 'The Count' Kennedy and so many more. These Brummies of character were joined by Sal the Salt Lady who traipsed the street flogging blocks of salt and by that great scion of working-class Brummagem, Holy Joe. Devoutly religious and desirous of helping those in need, especially children, this supposedly ordinary working chap collared tirelessly for the well being of working-class youngsters. A railwayman, he was well known in and around Duddeston, Bordesley, Small Heath and Saltley and also, of course, in the Bull Ring.

A few years back Sheila Guy wrote to me with her memories of Holy Joe. Back in her childhood years she lived in Gopsal Street, which was off Cardigan Street and Curzon Street. She said, 'My mother told me of Holy Joe's good works with the children of the area but I never went to his meetings. I remember Joe best of all as a chimney sweep! When my mother decided it was time for the chimney to have its annual clean, I was sent to Holy Joe`s house with a written message of when to come. He lived down Lawley Street, by Wright's Ropes and off I would go with the note. Then the operation chimney sweep would begin - pictures down, peg rug up, anything that could not be moved was covered with cloths, ornaments out of sight to be washed ready to be put back on the mantle.

'Mom was up very early that morning preparing all this and I would go to school, only to find when I got home at dinner-time that he hadn't been!! As he worked for the railway, it was probably a change of shift that caused him to let us down, but it invariably happened and then off I would go again with another note and another date was made. Regarding the lady who sang "Count your blessings" does anyone remember another small lady who used to come around the back streets of Brum singing "Glory for me, Glory for me, I shall look on His face. There will be glory, yes glory for me".'

This photo of Holy Joe (on the far right) was sent to me by Dorothy Lakin. Holy Joe was the grandfather 'of a friend of mine, Edie Greenhouse, now Mrs Coomes. We lived in Belmont Row, up the mission yard. Holy Joe lived at a yard called Portland Place in Lawley Street. Edie's mother, Mary nee Waite left behind these family photos, which Edie kindly lent me to copy and hand them over to you.' George Hinckley is the chap on the far left. He retired in 1967 after 43 years on the railway.

The photo brought back memories for Mr T. W. Allen because the famed preacher and raiser of funds for the poor was his mother's brother: 'her name was Emily Waite before she got married. Holy Joe used to visit us at Speedwell Road, Hay Mills. I was only a young lad at the time, but I can still remember him, his chimney sweeping, his railway and his home in Lawley Street and his preaching – hence his name Holy Joe. I'm glad other people remember him.'

Emma Bygrave also recalls Holy Joe and she has a wonderful recollection of other Brummagem characters such as the strong man in the Bull Ring and the woman 'who sang the Glory song. She used to come up Witton Road most Saturdays. Where she came from or where she was going I never knew. She used to sing, "Oh that will be Glowery for me", not Glory. She certainly was a poor soul. There was also an organ grinder who always stopped outside our shop on Witton Road. I think he had a monkey on top, but I'm not sure. It was a barrel organ.

'There was another man who came up Witton Road, he turned gambols outside Bird's greengrocers and Mr Bird would give him fruit. There was a little woman who pushed a basket carriage around selling blocks of salt. She supplied our shop and it was cut into brick sizes to sell. I remember the handy carrier woman too. There was a very respectable man, well dressed, who was blind. He played the concertina and stood under the bridge at Witton by Kynoch's as it was then. Another man I remember came up Witton Road, and he had a knife and scissors sharpener. He treadled it and the wheel went round. What a blessing we do not see these things now.'

Steven Corcoran balancing a 228lbs Wagon Wheel on his chin in Birmingham's Bull Ring. His son, Richard, recalls that his father was a travelling man: 'He had a big family of children and he travelled around, him and his brother Richard. I'm named after him and they put shows on for the public. My dad would swallow a pocket watch on a long chain and had a lot of people put their ear to his belly and listen to the tick. He'd also lie on a bed of nails and have a slab broken on his chest. He would also use a whip to take the ash from my mother's mouth while she would hold the cigarette in her mouth. He'd then remove the red cinder and then the cigarette last.

'He ripped the telephone books and escaped from chains and handcuffs while being tied up in a canvas bag. My uncle had many talents and would do his bit. My father had many brothers and at least 10 of them were show men. I believe my sister Winnie still has some of my father's flyers. My father was special and he could pull a crowd in and hold the attention. He had a gift. He loved people and people would listen and all show the man respect.'

A street entertainer about to perform 'the rope tying trick' on wasteland in Corporation Street in 1890.

Like many other people, Maureen Perks has 'lots of memories of the Bull Ring, the cobbled streets the hill to climb when entering the bottom of the Bull Ring passing the Smithfield Market, the variation of smells some very unpleasant some pleasant from cooking smells to scented from the fresh flowers.

'One of my most memorable was at the age of about five years old running along side my father marching up the Bull Ring in the Band of Territorial Army or the Royal Artillery. I am not sure which as my father was in both. He was at the front as he was a drummer and on occasions he would play solo. It was such a tremendous site with all the Bandsmen dressed in Red Uniforms with gold buttons and braids. The drum ropes gleaming white which my father had spent hours cleaning. I only wish I had a photograph of this. Perhaps with luck someone may send you one. I hope so.

'My mother used to take my brothers and me most Saturdays to shop for vegetables off the Barrow Boys. Our special treat was a bag of baked potatoes off the Black Carts and we used to love helping ourselves to the salt from the lift up lid the containers attached to the side of the casts. In the cold weather it was great to keep our hands warm.

'My brothers used to love watching the Escape Artist and I got my joy from watching my brothers' faces as their expressions changed from concern to amazement. The little lady who was blind and stood near the market hall selling Brown Handy Carriers her squeaky voice and she was always dressed in black.

I also remember a very glamorous lady on one of the barrows selling vegetables she had lots of Blonde Hair which she wore up on top and lots of make up and long Red Nails. How she managed to keep them so long I don't know.

'The hustle and bustle of the people trying to get the best buys and holding on to my mother's hand in case I got lost. I think it is sad that our Bull Ring has changed so much over the years. I also remember the policeman on horseback and having to dodge into the road to sometimes get past the pavements too crowded, making sure not to tread in anything the horses may have left behind.'

A Proper Brummie: Kathleen Dayus

Kathleen Dayus knew what it was to rough it. The thirteenth child of a poor family, she grew up in a yard in Camden Street on the edge of the Jewellery Quarter. In one of the most prosperous cities of one of the wealthiest counties in the world, the local folk had to collar and scrat for everything and anything they had. Like Kathleen's dad, many of the chaps were out of work and were on the parish, 'but what they received was insufficient to feed us growing children, let alone our parents as well'. Friday afternoons, the hard up and unemployed would queue for cards that allowed them a bit of coal, a loaf or two, some margarine, a tin of condensed milk, a little tea, and spoonful or so of sugar.

Court Number 7, Camden Grove off Camden Drive, about 1905. Thanks to Birmingham Library Services. Camden Street is a long street, beginning at The Parade and ending at Clissold Street, Brookfields. It is split into two by Icknield Street. Camden Drive lay at the top end of Camden Street, between Sloane Street and Albion Street and on the edge of the Jewellery Quarter. Narrow and short it ran into Legge Lane and is given as a separate entry in Kelly's Directory for 1911. Camden Grove came off Camden Street and also went in to Legge Lane. Kathleen went to Saint Paul's Church of England School which was in Camden Grove, although the Directories state it was in Camden Drive. She herself would have lived in a yard very close to the one shown in this photo.

This relief was grudging and meagre and money was never given. In their prejudice against the poor, too many of those in authority believed that poorer folk could not be trusted with cash in case they spent it on snuff, tobacco, beer or suchlike. Poverty was a hard bed. Kathleen and her pals knew what it was to be clammed and to stand outside the factory gates begging for a piece off the workers when they knocked off. And they knew what it was like to live in tiny houses that were badly built and to have to share insanitary dry-pan closets.

As if that wornt enough, Kathleen was treated harshly by her mom. Her was a tough woman who would bounce out of the house with the old mon's flat cap pushed firmly onto her head. In later years, Kathleen came to an understanding of why her mom was that way. It was life that had squeezed the affection from her and made her forbidding.

But the life that Kathleen and her pals lived wasn't one of unremitting unhappiness. They had their laughs, they played their games, they whistled and they sang and they made the best of the bed that they lay on. Like so many Brummies who come out the back streets, Kathleen was an intelligent and persevering woman. She wanted something better out of life and through heartaches that would have broken many a person, she forged on, holding fast to a dream of a better life for her kids and a better world for her grandkids. Determined and dogged, whenever life knocked her down her pulled herself back up, dusted herself and got on with it.

But Kathleen didn't just dream, she grafted to make her dream a reality. She saw her kids and grandkids – and her great grandkids – get on. But she never forgot her people. She never walked away from the working-class Brummies of the back streets and one day she set her mind to telling their tale, the tale of Her People. In 1982 the book of that name came out. It was written with the insight and understanding of someone who belonged and who had not forgotten her roots. *Her People* was brought out by a major London publisher. It gained national attention and Kathleen went on to Terry Wogan's show. Her down-to-earth Brummie ways grabbed the audience and made them sit up and take notice. So many people wrote in to hear more of her that they had fetch her back on.

Kathleen in 1933.

Through all the attention, Kathleen stayed the same and she wrote more books. These were also successful, but it was *Her People* that laid the ground for me and others to follow. Kathleen was the first. She was the first to recount the lives of those working-class Brummies who never had nothing from society but who gave so much. She was the pioneer and she inspired us. I was fortunate to know Kathleen well. Over fifteen years ago when I was struggling to make my way and when I had just come off the dole, she came and did a talk for me at my first teaching job. She didn't have to but she did because she wanted to help me. Kathleen was there for anyone who cared about all those Brummies whose address was back of.

A photo of Kathleen later in life.

Kathleen died just before we should have celebrated her 100th birthday and her family had asked me to say a few words. I was honoured. Kathleen, these are my words. If ever there was a Proper Brummie you were her. Because of you, your people will never be forgotten. I was proud to be your pal. God Bless, ma wench. Rest in peace, your work is done. You did it well.

The Good Knight of Deritend: Sir John Smedley-Crooke

The ordinary men and women of Birmingham acclaimed him as the Ex-Serviceman's MP, and his own constituents declared him to be the Good Knight of Deritend. He was Sir John Smedley-Crooke, a Member of Parliament who worked tirelessly and determinedly for all those men who had been prepared to give their lives for their country in the First World War – so many of whom had come back not to a Land Fit For Heroes but to unemployment, ill health and hard times. Quietly but doggedly, and often in association with the Royal British Legion, Sir John strove to help those who had not failed their country in its hour of need but who had been failed by their country in the peace that followed.

As MP for Deritend, where poverty was widespread, he put aside half of his parliamentary salary to form a fund out of which trustees helped deserving cases; he sponsored a bill to make compulsory the employment of former servicemen in the Civil Service; and he persistently and without show pushed forward claims for the pension rights of veterans. And in an innovative move, Sir John Smedley-Crooke initiated weekly interview sessions at which his constituents could come and discuss with him their problems. As he recalled, 'It was on a Friday. The House (of Commons) finished at four, so if I got the 4.30 I was here at my desk at Digbeth Institute at half-past six. In other words, whilst the House was sitting your Member was there to see you. I sometimes had as many as 30 interviews in an hour and a half and, the next week in Parliament, went into each individual case.' Sir John's initiative was quickly adopted over the country and today each MP as a matter of course offers weekly surgeries.

Born in 1861 in Matlock, he was educated at the Grammar School in Aldridge and Shoal Hill College, Cannock. Then, aged eighteen, he joined the Royal Warwickshire Volunteers, completing four years service. Later, between 1897 and 1905 he was with the Queen's Own Worcester Hussars (Imperial Yeomanry), and when war broke out in 1914 this man of 53 sought to do his bit. Turned down for active service, he tried and tried again. Finally accepting that he would not be able to fight, he was offered a commission and, stationed at Worcester, he was put in charge of the Substitution Department. Here Sir John ensured that fit men who were working in the factories would replace, substitute, unfit men in the military who in turn would move on to munitions work. His idea was taken up by the War Office and afterwards, Sir John moved on to become Munitions Area Substitution Officer, Birmingham.

With the coming of peace he was earning a good and sufficient income from his business of Crooke and Riley, pawnbroker's of High Street, Birmingham, to be able to concentrate on public service. He became honorary treasurer of the Midlands District of the Comrades of the Great War and of the Unity Relief Committee. This latter body began a canteen for men seeking work, where Sir John also inaugurated a kind of employment exchange. When the British Legion (as it was then) started in 1921, he

John Smedley-Crooke MP talking with a lady living in a back-to-back in Emily Street, Highgate. Thanks to the Birmingham Evening Mail.

Sir John chatting with residents in what looks like the Ashcroft Estate in Ashted in July 1938. Thanks to the Birmingham Evening Mail.

became honorary treasurer of the Birmingham County Council. A year later he was asked by the Conservatives locally to stand in the General Election for the staunchly working-class constituency of Deritend.

In the face of strong opposition from Labour and the Liberals, he won with an almost 5,000 vote majority. Subsequent elections were noted for the strong and close contests between Sir John and the Labour candidate, Fred Longdon, who wrested the seat away from the Conservatives in 1929. Two years later, it was reclaimed by Sir John. He held it until his retirement in 1945. Knighted in 1938, Sir John played a crucial role in the formation of the Home Guard, whose men carried out vital and distinguished service in the Second World War. He died in 1951, admired by all for his sincerity and championing of ex-servicemen and their rights.

Sir John Smedley-Crooke (second from left) marching in the Royal British Legion East Birmingham Church Parade in Watery Lane, Bordesley. Thanks to the Birmingham Evening Mail. Ivy MacGregor, nee Allison, was interested to read my article about Sir John Smedley-Crooke MP, as 'I worked for his agent, Mr Thomas Batty, for five years in the 1930s. Mr Batty is on Sir John's left hand side in the photograph, and the man on the right hand side was Councillor Joe White, a local man who lived in

Arthur Street, Small Heath. Sir John was a kind and generous man, who worked ceaselessly for the ex-servicemen and people of Deritend, whatever their political beliefs. His local headquarters was at 175, Deritend, a few doors from the "Old Crown". I spent five happy years working with Mr Batty at the Central Office in Edmund Street and still have the reference I received when I left in 1939.'

Seeing this shot brought Elsie Birks back to 'voting days when we were young and living in Ashley Street. I remember riding round on the back of a lorry shouting, "Vote, vote, vote for Percy Shurmer, Who's that knocking at the door, If it's Smedley and his wife we'll stab him with a knife and he won't come voting any more." Needless to say I wasn't old enough to know anything about what voting was about. Happy days. We loved Percy Shurmer's parties and his band.

'I've been reading about the back-to-back houses. We lived in a back to back in Ashley Street, one up, one down. There was just my Mom, Dad and sister Ada and myself. Didn't have much money but we never went without and I tell you we had some of the happiest days of our lives then. We kids had concerts at the back of the coal lorry. We lived at the back of Wilcock's coal merchants. My dear friend Rose lived in our yard, too, but they had two bedrooms.'

The Coldstreamers of Brum

With Kitchener to Khartoum

Why my great grandfather, Richard Chinn, joined the Coldstream Guards we don't know, but join them he did as a teenager – as would many Brummies, for the Coldstream Guards recruited strongly in Birmingham. Unfortunately, we know little about his service, although we do have a photo of him as one of the bearers for the funeral of the Duchess of Albany, as we thought. However it is more likely that he carried her husband, Prince Leopold, the Duke of Albany and the youngest son of Queen Victoria who died in March 1884.

The other scrap of information we have is that we were told that my great granddad was in the relief column that was sent to rescue General Gordon who was besieged in Khartoum, the capital of the Sudan. This country was mostly in the hands of rebels against Egyptian rule headed by a religious leader, the Mahdi. Egypt itself had been occupied by British troops since 1882 following the victory at Tel-el-Kabir in 1882. In fact, the 2nd Battalion of the Coldstream Guards had been part of a Guards Brigade in that battle under the command of Sir Garnet Wolseley. From County Carlow in Ireland, he was the older brother of Frederick York Wolseley who invented the mechanical sheep shearer. Wolseley's company later employed Herbert

My great grandfather Richard Chinn is standing second from the right on this photograph showing him in his uniform as a Coldstreamer.

Austin and from the end of the nineteenth century its base was the Sydney Works in Alma Street, Aston.

In late 1884, after a massive campaign by the national newspapers, the British Government sent Lord Wolseley, as he now was, to lead an army to relieve Gordon. Wolseley quickly formed a Camel Corps to strike out across the desert towards Khartoum and give moral support to Gordon. A picked force, it included volunteers from the Guards regiments, amongst whom were men of the 1st and 2nd battalions the Coldstream Guards. It seems one them was my great grandfather.

Led by Colonel Stewart, the Camel Corps of just over 2,000 men came up against the 11,000 strong enemy on 16 January 1885 at the wells of Abu Klea. Stewart formed a zereba, an entrenched camp, which was fired upon throughout the night. The next morning he advanced in a hollow square, with the Guards and Mounted Infantry at the front. The Sudanese attacked the square fiercely and broke through the rear.

After a few minutes mayhem, the rear reformed and the enemy was repulsed bloodily. Amongst the British killed was Colonel Burnaby, a staunch Conservative who had stood for Parliament against Joe Chamberlain in Birmingham in 1880 and to whom there is a monument in Saint Philip's Churchyard. An obelisk in Portland stone, it is over 50 feet high. At its base is a relief portrait of Burnaby in uniform, whilst there are carvings of military regalia and the names and dates of his campaigns at Khiva in 1875 and Abu Klea.

The Camel Corps moved on and soon after was attacked again by the Sudanese, who as before showed great bravery. Colonel Stewart was killed, but now commanded by Sir Charles Wilson, the Camel Corps pressed through its opponents towards the Nile. They came upon four of Gordon's steamers and were handed a letter from the beleaguered general. It was dated 14 December and declared, 'I think the game is up'. Sadly it was.

On 24 January Wilson set off on a steamer down the Nile with a small bodyguard to find out what was happening in Khartoum. It was too late. They reached the outskirts of the town and realised it had fallen. On 26 January, the Mahdi's men had breached the defences. Gordon and all his troops were killed, as were thousands of the town's folk who had not fled previously and surrendered into slavery. I wished that my Great Grandad Richard had passed on more about of his experiences as a Coldstreamer and that I knew how he felt about the mission to save Gordon.

An Old Contemptible

The Kaiser thought his great army would sweep in to the sea that small force of British soldiers sent to help the French when war with Germany broke out on 4 August 1914. So sneering was he of the British Expeditionary Force that he commanded his forces to 'exterminate first the treacherous English and walk over General French's contemptible little army'. Massively outnumbered, yet the gallant British regulars were not overwhelmed. They proved to be tough and dogged opponents, who were skilled and swift marksmen with their Lee Enfields. My Grandad, Private Richard

Alfred Chinn number 9968, 2nd Battalion Coldstream Guards was one of those men who proudly called themselves the Old Contemptibles after the war.

He arrived in France on 13 August as part of the 4th (Guards) Brigade in the 2nd Division of I Corps. Five days later he wrote to his Mom in Alfred Street, Sparkbrook, 'We start this morning Tuesday for the front, sent out with rations and 120 rounds of ammunition each. Don't know wear we are for just yet let know later if we can. I don't think it will last long we are a happy Battalion of men and that's what the Germans are not. England for ever.'

On 23 August the 2nd battalion crossed the Belgian border. By now Grandad and his pals were part of the 1st (Guards) Brigade in the newly-formed Guards Division, along with the 3rd Coldstreams, 2nd Grenadiers and 1st Irish. That day at the Battle of Mons the British showed their mettle, but faced with massive German superiority in numbers they had to retreat. Most of the heavy fighting involved troops of II Corps, which included the 1st Battalion Coldstream Guards; but soon the 2nd Battalion was involved in some big and important battles. After the French with British support pushed back the Germans at the Battle of the Marne in early September, the BEF locked horns with the enemy at the Battle of the Aisne. This began the trench warfare that so characterised the British experience of the First World War.

My Grandad, Guardsman Richard Chinn, third from the left and in the chair in a convalescent home in South Wales following his wounding at La Bassé early in 1915.

During that battle Grandad let his Mom know that he was still alive and well, although 'we are having a rough time at present it has done nothing but rain for 5 days we have had plenty to do out here I will shake hands with myself if I get back in England after this, chaps who where in the south Africa said it was nothing to this we are at it every day here. General French congratulated us on our the Guards work what we have done'. A few days later Grandad urged his Mother not 'to worry about me if it is my luck to go I go if not I live to tell the tale about it, we take no more notice of it than working in a factory it is our work we have got used to it.'

By early October the British forces were in Flanders, where for a month until 18 November, I Corps fought the bloody and bitter 1st Battle of Ypres. Five days before its end, Grandad told of a how his 'arms ached through shooting so much and quick' in repulsing one German attack. After the battle he proudly recounted how other soldiers declared that 'there's no fear of Germans breaking through the lines when we are there, I saw in the paper a regiment were 9 days in the trenches we were <u>25</u> days and in half a <u>foot of water</u> at that.'

There was a chap from Highgate Road in Grandad's company and a Brummie lad he knew, G. Carpenter, was wounded at Ypres. Another chum, Jim Dear, was in the 1st Battalion Coldstream Guards who 'were out here before us, one of the first regiments to come out, they been all through it from Mons to this last place and done plenty of fighting to, I think the Brigade of Guards have done their share of fighting and still some more left to carry on with, more than the Germans care for I am afraid.' Grandad was right.

Soon after the 1st Battle of Ypres, Our Grandad was put in the Machine Gun Section of the 2nd Battalion of the Coldstream Guards. In mid December, he wrote to his Mom asking her what his Dad thought 'of his old regiment they have not done bad I think they are keeping there good name up, I read in a paper of the Germans throwing a bomb in our trenches that did not explode in which an officer threw it back again an this time it did go off amongst the Germans, well it was done by our Officer in charge of the Machine Gun Sec'.

By now the battalion was 'rested' in routine marches and refitting. Then on 22 December, it set out for the trenches, which were in a terrible state owing to the continual rain. That Christmas was uncomfortable as the problems posed by the deep mud were worsened by heavy shelling from the Germans. Many men were killed on Christmas Day itself. Our Grandad wrote to his Mom on 4 January that 'we look like if we had a cartload of mud tipped on us, but the boys keep on smiling'. His officer bought the lads a concertina and 'when we go in the barns we have a little concert'.

A few days later Grandad recounted how 'you have heard of the Germans and English being friends on Christmas Day, it was different in the trenches were the 4th Guards Brigade was for if you put your head above the trench you where a goner also if a German done the same his number would be up'. As Grandad declared, 'we were the Guards Brigade where we was out to fight not to play with them as they have found'. That letter was finished 'good old Blues hard luck with the Villa'.

At the end of January the Battalion moved to the brickfields at La Bassé. Sometime in February, Grandad was wounded badly in the knee joint and transferred to the Western and General Hospital, in Cardiff. On 18 March he told his Mom that 'I shall be glad to see some of the old faces around the brook (Sparkbrook), but there will be a few missing who laid down their lives for England'. Grandad's wound was too bad to allow him to go to back to the Front and eventually he came back to the Brook. When he died I was too young to have asked him questions. Luckily he left his letters so we know something of his war-time experiences and I know this: I am proud to be the grandson of an Old Contemptible.

My Grandad is second from the left on the third table from the front, and to the left is my Great Grandad, another old Coldstreamer. We think this is a meeting of the Birmingham Branch of the Coldstream Guards Association in the 1930s. Does anyone recognise anyone else?

A Proud Coldstreamer

Things were rather hot, that night in late January 1915 when Wal Eden and his section from 2nd Battalion the Coldstream Guards found themselves isolated in front of the British lines at the brickfields of La Bassé. As he recalled years later in a typical understatement, 'it was a bit of a do there'. The Germans were in a strong defensive position, both in trenches and behind stacks of bricks. Sections from the Coldstream Guards and the Irish Guards were sent from the British trenches, to snipe at the enemy and throw grenades at them. Wal's section of sixteen was amongst them and had come under fierce attack.

Six of his comrades were Brummagem lads, including Sergeant Black, Ben Lippitt and a chap called Harris. Unfortunately all three were killed. Things looked rough and so the Corporal looked at his remaining men and said, 'One of you has to go back and see what's got to be done.' Wal volunteered. Although there was some moonlight, it was mostly pitch black. Wal began to make his way back to the reserve trench to find his officers and the rest of the company and to get orders. Bullets were whizzing around him and then he heard someone groan. A voice in an Irish accent said, 'They've got me in the back and legs. Can you help me?'

Reared as one of eleven kids in Nechells, Wal knew all about giving and having to help out others with no thought of reward. He did no more but put down his rifle and picked up the Irish feller. At 5 foot 10 and a half, Wal was a very strong bloke and taking no heed of the danger he carried his wounded comrade fifty-odd yards back to the reserve trench. As he approached, the sentry called out, 'Halt! Who goes there!' Wal replied, 'Private Eden, Coldstream Guards, with a wounded man.'

Told to come in, Wal informed Captain Bennett of the situation of his section. The officer answered, 'Well, if you can't hold on, you'd better come back.' Then he noticed Wal had no rifle and asked where it was. When Wal explained that he had put it down to rescue the wounded soldier, the Captain was angered, although he was mollified a little when he was informed, 'There's plenty more rifles I can pick up on my way back'.

Returning to his section, Wal then came back with them to the safety of his company. A day or so later, on 1 February, Lance Corporal O'Leary of the Irish Guards won his famous VC when the Coldstreamers and Irish Guards were ordered to assault the German trenches. Running swiftly across 150 yards of No Man's Land, he outstripped his company, killed five Germans of a machine gun position and then killed another three. My Grandad, Alf Chinn was a pal of Wal Eden and was also in the 2nd Battalion Coldstream Guards. He was in action that day and saw O'Leary's bravery.

Later that year, Wal was gassed at the Battle of Loos (September/October 1915). With no gas masks, the British troops were issued with a drop of liquid that they had to pour over a piece of flannel and then hold over their faces in the event of a gas attack. There was not time to do this. The Germans exploded a form of tear gas, and Wal was affected badly in his stomach, 'but the biggest trouble was the eyes. I was more or less blinded. My eyes were running all the while."

After recovering in the 3rd Canadian General Hospital, Wal rejoined the 2nd Battalion in January 1916. Within six months he had been badly wounded. On sentry duty between two outposts ahead of the British trenches, he spotted three or four Germans approaching. Wal remembered what happened: 'I knew that none of our fellers was out. Naturally I let fly at them. I had one of them shot. Next thing I was lying back in the trenches. They'd thrown a bomb at me. It shattered my arm and a clod of earth blinded me for a few days.'

Eventually discharged from the Army, Wal was awarded a 60% pension worth 13s 9d a week. I was honoured to have met Wal when in the twilight of his life he told me of his friendship with my Grandad. Both of them were proud to be Brummie Coldstreamers.

Ex-Guardsman Wal J. Eden, 2nd Battalion Coldstream Guards. Wal served with the Regiment from 22 July 1912 until he was discharged on 9 February 1917 as the result of severe wounds received at Saint Julien, near Ypres in Belgium several months previously. Thanks to Wal's proud relative, Ken Bladon.

Nulli Secundus

Jim Hetherington has dropped me a note about his service with the Coldstream Guards. His story begins at the Guards Depot at Caterham in 'August 1943. There I was a recruit, also there was Frank Goldsby. Frank and I were born in Emily Street, Balsall Heath. We both did our training at the Depot, then onto the Training Battalion at Pirbright. At least 17 weeks hard infantry training, then Frank and I went on to the 5th Battalion Infantry. I went on to the Guards Armoured Training Wing and had several weeks training as a wireless operator till I was sent to Europe. I was on my way, embarked on a corvette Navy ship, and although I was 22 years old it was the first time I had seen the sea.

'We arrived at Dieppe, got off the ship to be met by several hundred German prisoners. I thought the war must be over, but it was not so. We then travelled in dark, uncomfortable cattle trucks to Holland. There we slept under hedges in a transit camp till we were taken to our respective battalions. I did various jobs as a spare crewman till in 1945 I was posted to a Sherman 17 pounder tank (a tank destroyer). Then on March 9th 1945 our Squadron No 1 and Frank Goldsby's Company in the 5th Battalion set off at 1400 HRS to break the German Army's 7th Parachute Regiment's hold on the crossing of the Rhine.

'The Coldstream Guards won this battle against all odds where other Divisions had failed. Once again Frank and I were close to each other, in fact our tank 4 Charlie No. 4 Troop No 1 Squadron was instrumental in destroying a German machine gun nest in

No. 3 Company, 1st Battalion Coldstream Guards, December 1947 at Pirbright prior to going to Palestine. This was Jim Hetherington's Company and also that of my Uncle Ron. I wish to thank Jim and all the other members of the Coldstream Guards Association Birmingham Branch for their help in researching these articles on the Coldstreamers and also for their friendship. I am proud and honoured to know you all.

a building called Hausloo, but victory was ours and Frank and I survived. After that I carried on to further incidents and the end of the War at Cuxhaven. There the 7th Parachute Regiment of the German Army would only surrender to the Guards Armoured Division.

'Frank had been wounded in the latter days of the war. I carried on till 1946 in B.A.O.R. (British Army on the Rhine) and then came home to service in England. In 1947 I was posted to the Training Battalion as a Physical Training Instructor where I was made Lance/Sergeant (another story). While I was there one of the Army Physical Training Instructors was Bill Nankeville, Bobby Davro's father, who also ran for England.

'For a few months I was content, but then the 1st Battalion came to Pirbeck, prior to going to Palestine. I could not let them go without me, so after a lot of discussion I went back to 3 Company 1st Battalion Coldstream Guards. Then after extensive training off to Palestine and who should be one of the Guardsmen in my platoon but Buck Chinn's brother, your Uncle Ron Chinn. But that is another story.

'So briefly now, Palestine – East Africa, Tripoli, North Africa, back home in 1949, public duties and then my 7 years was nearly up. Demobbed, one week to go then called back to Wellington Barracks in London, off again to Tripoli, a few months there then on to the Canal Zone (Tel-el-Kebir). Then after 8½ years service back home to my 2nd Demob. But once a Coldstreamer always a members of the Coldstream Guards. Nulli Secundus – Second to None.'

Athelstan. Our Great Leader

He overthrew the Danish kingdom of York, he was the first leader to hold sway over all of the English, and he was proclaimed as 'rex totius Britanniae', king of all Britain. His name was Athelstan. He reigned over England from 924 until 939 and he spoke the Anglo-Saxon dialect of the West Mercians, the dialect from which is drawn crucial elements in the accent and speech of working-class Brummagem.

Athelstan's achievements were wide-ranging and impressive. He was both a cunning warleader and a noted lawgiver. In 937 he overwhelmed an alliance of Scots, Welsh, Scandinavians and Irish at the battle of Brunanburh, but within the bounds of his lands all men - irrespective of their backgrounds - were treated equally under his codes of law. One of the greatest of all the Anglo-Saxon kings, he was given due honour by the leading rulers of Western Europe and he is recognised now as one of the most important figures in the emergence of England as a nation.

The grandson of King Alfred the Great and the son of Edward the Elder, Athelstan came of the House of Wessex, the kingdom that dominated southern England and which survived the attacks of the Danes which destroyed all the other Anglo-Saxon

Hay making on Frogmill Farm, Northfield, then in Worcestershire, about 1900. The farm is recalled in Frogmill Road.

kingdoms. But though he was a southerner through his father's line, he was a West Mercian by upbringing.

Back in the late 870s, the Vikings had captured eastern Mercia, but they failed to wrest from the Anglo-Saxons what became Warwickshire, Worcestershire, Staffordshire, Herefordshire, Shropshire, Cheshire and southern Lancashire. This West Mercian area came under the sway of Earldorman Aethelred, who married Alfred's sister, Lady Aethelflaed. Known as the Lady of the Mercians, she ruled in her own right after her husband's death in 911 and was responsible for establishing a number of boroughs, fortresses, to defend her lands from the Danes. Amongst these were Tamworth and Stafford in 913 and Warwick in 914. Aethelflaed also fought with her brother, Edward the Elder the king of Wessex, against the Scandinavians and together they gained a noteworthy victory at the battle of Tettenhall, near Wolverhampton, in about 910.

It was Aethelflaed and Earldorman Aethelred who brought up Athelstan because King Alfred had been keen to ensure that the west Mercians were not treated as a subject people and would have one of his blood as one of their own. It is also believed that Alfred's mother was a Mercian as was his mother-in-law. With a West Mercian upbringing and education, Athelstan was proclaimed king by his West Mercian friends in 924, following the death of his father and the sudden death of his brother who was the heir to the throne. It was a momentous decision with deep ramifications for the development of England.

Reared in our region and as king of all England, Athelstan spoke as a West Mercian. This was an Anglo-Saxon dialect that would have been understood by his subjects in the south and north but which had distinctive features. Unfortunately, there survive very few texts written in the Mercian dialect. However, those that do remain indicate that the Mercians turned an 'a' into an 'o' before a nasal consonant such as 'n', 'm' and 'ng'. Thus Mercians would have said mon for man, hond for hand and lond for land, and this feature has led us Brummies to have moms as opposed to northern mams. It is remarkable that this form of speech has survived so strongly into the twenty-first century in Birmingham and the Black Country.

As well as having this specific pronunciation, it is most likely that despite the passage of over 1,000 years, Athelstan would have known what

Court 17 in Hospital Street in the Summer Lane neighbourhood, about 1905. Thanks to Birmingham Library Services.

In yards such as these and in profoundly urban and industrial setting, working-class Brummies kept alive the dialect of West Mercia and used words like miskins that dated back to Anglo-Saxon times, and others such as suff which Shakespeare used.

modern Brummies are talking about when they refer to the miskins - for that word for dustbins is derived from the West Mercian 'mixen' which meant dung and thence dung heap and rubbish heap. So when you hear someone say 'Marry the miskin for the muck and get pisened by it', you'll know that anyone who marries for money will regret it.

Similarly, when you're told 'to pack up yer blartin else I will gie y summat to blart about', you're using the West Mercian word blaetan, signifying the bleating of sheep - and from that comes the meaning of blarting to cry. There are other words that connect us with the origins of the English language in our region. Amongst them is clammed for hungry, from clemmen and one of the many of our words also used by Shakespeare - in this case in Scene IV of *The Winter's Tale* when he writes 'Clam your tongues and not a word more', indicating that the people should starve their tongues of words. The Bard also uses wench in the sense that we would do in Brum as a term of endearment and not as something derogatory - for in Scene II of Act V of *The Taming of the Shrew* he penned the line 'Why there's a wench, come on and kiss me Kate'.

The speech of Brummagem has a long and honourable history. Let us not cast it into the miskin of the past, nor let our children be clammed of its richness.

John Izod and his family outside Grove Farm, Sparkhill in 1895. The photo was taken by Mrs Fanny H. Walker of 58, Camp Hill. Thanks to Birmingham Library Services. The farm was owned by the Greswolds, a family of some note in the Arden district of

north Warwickshire. Based in Kenilworth and Solihull, where they are brought to mind by the 'Greswolde Arms' in Knowle, they moved into Yardley in the early fifteenth century, buying a farm of 38 acres in 1420/1. Then in 1447/8 a deed of release of the manor of Gretehurst in Yardley and land and tenements in Lichfield was entered into between Aymer Holt, esquire, and Thomas Greswold. However, the ownership of Greethurst was later disputed by the Holts and was regained by them in the early sixteenth century. By now the Greswolds owned at least four other properties in Yardley, and their holdings grew in the following years.

When Henry VIII dissolved the monasteries and other religious bodies, he took over their land and then sold it. The Greswolds profited from this process by purchasing Grove Farm, which had been owned by Maxstoke Priory and which is remembered in Grove Road, Springfield. The farmhouse stood close to the Stratford Road, between Grove Road and Greswolde Road. Lords of Greet Manor, the Greswoldes were also lay rectors of Yardley, hence Greswolde Road, Yardley, off Station Road and almost opposite Vicarage Road; and also Greswolde Park Road, Acocks Green, off the Warwick Road. The Greswolds owned Grove Farm until it was sold for building in 1896 by an heir who added an 'e' to the end of his name.

Despite the presence of Irish, Welsh, Scots, Jewish, Italian and German folk in nineteenth-century Birmingham, the vast majority of Brummies were English – and of them the majority were either incomers from Warwickshire, Worcestershire and Staffordshire or else were descended from rural people from those counties who had moved to Birmingham. This meant that the dialect of Birmingham was embedded within that of its rural hinterland – and of course, that dialect was infused with words from Anglo-Saxon and Middle English.

Artist Made in Brum

It was a tragedy, which Edward Jones never got over. He'd already lost his first child, a little girl, but to have his wife taken away within a week of the birth of his son in 1833 was a burden too heavy to be borne. For the rest of his life he mourned deeply the wife he had loved so dearly. Each Sunday he would take his lad with him to worship at St Mary's, the Anglican church deep in the Gun Quarter at Whittall Street and they they'd make the sorrowful walk to the well-tended grave.

In silent melancholy this youngster, Edward Burne Jones watched a scene which seared itself into his soul. His dad would kneel by the stone of commemoration, his head bent forward and his shoulders throbbing with sobs which wracked his mind and spirit as much as his body. Sometimes as he stood up from his weeping he would grab his son's hand, squeezing it so tightly in his desolation that it made the lad cry out in pain.

For all his grief, Edward Jones did not abandon his son. A frame maker, carver and guilder by trade he worked from his home at 11 Bennett's Hill – a new and posh part of town. Just a generation before, sheaves of corn had swayed in the wind there and lads had run up its slopes to pick blackberries, but now it was laid out with fine buildings like the Corinthian style offices of the Birmingham Banking Company. Jones lived in a house hard on the left as you begin to stride up from New Street – and although later writers have said he was not successful in his business he must have been making a decent living to be able to afford such accommodation. He also managed to take on a housekeeper, Miss Sampson, who cooked cleaned and fetched and carried for him and his son.

While his feet were stood firmly in the soil of Brum, Edward Jones always seemed to have an other-worldly feel about him. He was 'tender hearted and touching' and 'believed all good things that were ever said of anyone'. There was no doubt that his pious nature made him quite unfit for the world into which he was pitched and though it has never been acknowledged it is inconceivable that his gentle and emotional approach to life did not have a profound effect both on the attitudes and art of his son.

Edward Burne Jones hinted at such himself. He recalled that there were few books in his childhood home but those that were present were all by poets. When the youngster was about twelve his father 'used to read to me little poems he made himself in a moving melodious and pathetic voice'. His tone proclaimed that he believed fervently in everything he recited, his sentiments and sensitivity perhaps a dual legacy from his Welsh ancestors. Throughout his distinguished career, Edward Burne Jones never heard readings delivered so sympathetically – and although as time went on his dad grew shy of speaking his verses, their influence lingered.

So too, did other actions of the older man. He may not have been interested in art and not have taken his son to concerts, but he had a passion for nature. If it could be seen, he would not miss a sunrise – dragging himself tiredly from his bed so as to wonder at one of God's gifts. And despite his weariness from work and his daily mourning, many's the time he walked miles to see a field of corn, taking his son with him to gaze at the unvarnished splendour of such a sight. It has been said that there was no beauty in his

Edward Burne Jones at work on the 'Star of Bethlehem', about 1884, from a photograph by Miss Barbara Leighton. Thanks to the Birmingham Evening Mail.

house and that he stifled his son's innate creativity. How could that be when he raised his child's spirit with his words, his actions, his beliefs, his love and his character?

A delicate boy and small for his age, at the age of eleven, Edward Burne Jones was sent by his father to be taught at King Edwards School – lower down New Street, where the Odeon now stands. Like most kids he had to make a stand against a bully, flying at his tormentor 'like a dog and then it was all over'. And, like many others he drew on the inspiration of one teacher in particular. Although liable to beat his boys for any infringement of discipline, Mr Abraham Thompson was able to do wondrous things with his language; 'with the flattest sentence in the world he would take us to ocean waters and the marshes of Babylon and the hills of Caucasus and the wilds of Tartary and the constellations and the abysses of space'.

Young Edward had entered the school in its commercial department, where he was to be prepared for a career in business or commerce, but it is obvious that he had impressed Mr Thompson. The teacher recommended to his father that Edward should be allowed to go on to the classical department. If his father had been mean spirited or unsuccessful, as has been presumed, he would never have agreed. For further education ensured a double financial expense: not only did it cost money but also it meant a wage lost – and then there was the extra expense of classes in design which the boy attended three evenings a week.

Gulping down books on history, romance and fable, the young Edward became fascinated with Celtic Stories and myths after reading Macpherson's Ossian. Such tales extolling the deeds of heroes and heroines raced through his mind and there can be doubt they profoundly affected his artistry. So, too, did the growing movement which sought to take the church back to its roots in the Middle Ages.

In particular Burne Jones felt the force of John Henry Newman – a leading member of the Church of England who converted to Catholicism and set up the Birmingham Oratory. Coming from an Evangelical Protestant background, Burne Jones did not go to mass and he never met Newman – but the magnetic priest had a sway over the young Brummie. He later

'The Star of Bethlehem'. Thanks to Birmingham Museum and Art Gallery. The painting was commissioned by Birmingham's Art Gallery Purchase Fund Committee. Burne-Jones began the painting in 1888. It is a large watercolour with life-size figures whose costumes glow. The artist declared that his painting would be 'a blaze of colour and look like a carol'. Using steps to achieve his work of art he exclaimed that he had 'journeyed as many miles already as ever kings travelled'.

recalled that in an age of 'sofas and cushion' Newman 'taught me to be indifferent to comfort, and in an age of materialism he taught me to venture into the unseen.'

Impressed by his son's talent, Mr Jones was determined that his lad should go to Oxford. The older man rented out his house in Bennett's Hill, took a smaller property on the Bristol Road and brought in a lodger to further help draw in funds. Disappointed by the university, Burne Jones never took his degree but was pulled into the group of Pre-Raphaelite artists focused on Dante Gabriel Rossetti. Then in 1861, and as a designer of tapestries and stained glass, he joined the celebrated firm of William Morris.

Within a few Years Edward Burne Jones had gained a high reputation not only as a craftsman but as an artist of talent drawing on Arthurian themes and Greek Fables. His works became world famous and some can be seen in our own Art Gallery, while Saint Philip's and Saint Martin's are enhanced by examples of his magnificent stained glass windows. Most critics have neglected the influence of Brum on this great artist. It is a mistake to do so. The poetry and pathos of his father, the verve and vision of Abraham Thompson, the spirituality and sensibility of John Henry Newman and the techniques and talents of his design teachers – all these ensured that the paintings and stained glass windows of Edward Burne Jones carried the mark of Birmingham.

'Love Among the Ruins' by Sir Edward Burne-Jones. Thanks to the Birmingham Evening Mail. This painting is on display at Wightwick Manor, bought in 1887 by Theodore Mander, the noted Wolverhampton manufacturer. Standing in the great parlour of what is now a National Trust property, the painting shows a man and a woman among the overgrown ruins of a palace which has wild roses entangled around the masonry. The sitter for the male figure was Gaetano Meo, an Italian mosaic worker who was a favourite model for the Pre-Raphaelites.

Conspicuous Valour. Brummie Heroes

Thomas George Turrall was a Brummie hero of whom we should be proud and about whom our children should be taught. Born in Hay Mills and in later life residing at 23, Oakley Road, Small Heath, Thomas Turrall joined the Worcestershire Regiment in the First World War and gained the highest honour for bravery in the British Army when he was awarded the Victoria Cross in 1916 during an action at La Boiselle

Whilst under fire on 3 July, Private Turrell rescued his wounded officer and carried him to a shell hole where the two of them stayed for three hours. Thomas George Turrall then carried his injured comrade back to safety during a British counter attack on the German lines. The Brummie distinguished himself during the terrible Battle of the Somme, on the first day of which on 1 July 1916, over 57,000 British soldiers became casualties.

In total, ten Brummies were honoured with the Victoria Cross between 1914 and 1918. Amongst them were Major (acting Lieutenant Colonel) John Neville Marshall MC, late of the Irish Guards and attached to the 16th Battalion Lancashire Fusiliers. An Acocks Green man, he showed conspicuous bravery, determination and leadership in the attack on the Sambre-Oise Canal on 4 November, 1918. On the same day and in a nearby action, similar qualities were displayed by Captain (acting Major) Arnold Horace Santo Waters, DSO, MC of the Royal Engineers. Although born in Plymouth, Arnold Waters was associated with Four Oaks in Sutton Coldfield.

Second Lieutenant H. James VC from Edgbaston was the final officer amongst the Birmingham men who gained the VC in the First World War. Serving with the 4th Battalion the Worcestershire Regiment, Second Lieutenant James was awarded the Victoria Cross for most conspicuous bravery during the Gallipoli campaign. On 28 June, 1915 and under his own initiative, he gathered a unit to support another part of the regiment - all of the officers of which had been killed during an attack. Under heavy shell and rifle fire, Second Lieutenant James went forward to the aid of his comrades and then returned with another group. According to his citation, 'his gallant example put fresh life into the attack'.

Soon after, on July 3, Second Lieutenant James led a group of bomb throwers up a Turkish communication trench. After nearly all his men had been killed or wounded, he remained alone at the head of the trench and 'kept back the enemy single-handed till a barrier had been built behind him and the trench secured'. Throughout this time, James was exposed to 'murderous fire'.

Three of the other Brummie Victoria Cross holders were sergeants. Ladywood-born Alfred Joseph Knight of the London Regiment was involved in several single-handed actions in which he captured enemy machine gun posts and a farm house on 20 September 1917 at Ypres. Norman Augustus Finch, of Handsworth and the Royal Marine Artillery, continued to fire his Lewis Gun from the foretop of HMS 'Vindictive' despite his severe wounds and thus saved the lives of many of his comrades on 22/23 July 1918. And Albert Gill of the King's Royal Rifle Corps was posthumously awarded the VC for his actions on 27 July 1916 at Delville Wood on the Western Front.

That day the Germans made a very strong attack on the right flank of Albert's battalion and succeeded in rushing the bomb post and killing all of the Company Bombers. Sergeant Gill rallied the remnants of his platoon, none of whom were skilled bombers, and reorganized their defences. This was a most difficult and dangerous task because the British trench was very shallow and much damaged. Soon afterwards, the enemy crept through the thick undergrowth, surrounded Sergeant Gill's men and began sniper fire from about 20 yards' range. Although it was almost certain death, Albert stood up boldly to direct the fire of his men. Sergeant Gill was killed

Sergeant Albert Gill. Thanks to David Delderfield.

almost at once but he allowed his men to hold up the enemy advance and so saved a very dangerous situation. There is a memorial to Sergeant Gill where he had worked, at the Post Office in Key Hill, Hockley

Two more of the bravest of the brave were lance corporals. The first was Lance Corporal Alfred Wilcox of the Oxford and Buckinghamshire Light Infantry, who led attacks which captured four enemy machine gun posts. From Aston, Alfred gained his honour on 12 September 1914 near Laventie, France. The second was Lance Corporal Amey. Serving with the 1/8th Royal Warwickshire Regiment, Amey from Duddeston won the VC on November 4, 1918, just days before the end of the war. During the attack on Landrecies, a heavy fog meant that the leading British troops were not able to 'mop up' a number German machine gun positions. Losing touch with his company, Amey attached his section to another which was held up by heavy machine gun fire from the enemy.

On his own initiative, he led his section in an attack on a machine gun nest. Despite the fierce fire from the Germans, 'with great bravery he forced the garrison to retire to a neighbouring farm, causing them to capitulate, and capturing about 50 prisoners and several machine guns'. Following this, the valiant Brummie single-handedly attacked another machine gun post in another farm house: 'exposed to heavy fire, he advanced unhesitatingly, killed two of the garrison and drove the remainder into a cellar until assistance arrived'.

Lance Corporal Amey's gallantry was not ended. On his own, he attacked a heavily-defended chateau in Fauborg Soyers which was holding up the line of advance. With 'determination and disregard of personal safety, he rushed the chateau, killed two Germans and held up the remainder till reinforced'. A further twenty prisoners were captured and the last opposition in the sector was cleared away. It was declared that Lance Corporal Amey's conduct had been of the highest type and was beyond praise.

The ranks of Birmingham's holders of the VC from The First World War are made up by Private Arthur Vickers VC of the Royal Warwickshire Regiment. His courageous act was at the Battle of Loos. On 25 September 1915 the 2nd Royal Warwicks valorously rushed from their trenches at half-past six in the morning. Battling through a terrible wave of fire, they

Lance Corporal W. Amey, VC MM, thanks to Dave Vaux.

reached the first German trenches at the Hulloch Quarries - but they found that the thick barbed wire which protected the enemy lines had not been cut as it should have been by the British bombardment which had preceded the assault.

Arthur Vickers was one of only four men in his company who had been issued with heavy and cumbersome wire cutters. With his mates falling all around him, Arthur took matters into his own hands. Instead of lying down to try and cut the wire and so give himself some protection, he stood up to allow himself more leverage.

It was broad daylight and he was within 50 yards of the Germans, but as he told his sister, Amy Atkins of Park Road, Aston, 'I had to use both my hands until there was no more use in them'. Arthur managed to cut two paths through the thickets of barbed wire and enabled his battalion to pass through and capture the first and second lines of the German trenches. Unhappily, later that day the Warwicks had to pull back because they were exposed through the withdrawal of British troops on their flanks.

That midnight on September 25, the Second Royal Warwicks presented themselves for muster. There were no officers left to take their names and out of a total of 523 men who had gone out to battle that morning, only 140 could call out. The rest were dead, wounded or missing in action. The casualties would have been even higher without the pluck of Arthur Vickers.

For his defiant spirit and outstanding bravery, Arthur Vickers was awarded the Médaille Militaire by the French and the Victoria Cross by the British. He was the first of six men from the Royal Warwicks to receive this the highest of his own country's accolades. Two months later, Arthur was honoured by his own City.

Although unable to be present at the ceremony in Victoria Square at which Lieutenant James VC was also honoured, Arthur's courage was made plain by Alderman Neville Chamberlain, the Lord Mayor. Birmingham's first citizen declared that there can have been few acts which were finer than that performed by Lance-Corporal Vickers for 'in the face of almost certain death, he voluntarily went out in murderous shell and rifle-fire, and cut the barbed wire which was holding up his battalion'.

John King tells me that of these valiant men, Alfred Wilcox lies in an unmarked grave. He feels that this is shameful on the city and that there should be a monument to all of the brave Brummie VC holders and also a display area devoted to them in the Museum and Art Gallery. I agree wholeheartedly.

Sergeant Clarence Steane of the Royal Warwickshire Regiment won the Military Medal during the Battle of the Somme in July 1916, when he showed conspicuous bravery in holding a barricade in a captured enemy trench, despite repeated German counter attacks. He was then wounded on 18 August and two days later wrote to his mother and father, telling them not to worry. On 22 August a telegram arrived at the family home in Bromsgrove Street stating that Clarence was very ill and that if they were able to make it, his parents could visit him at the Number 18 General Hospital in France. Sadly, on 24 August Clarence died of his wounds. He never knew that he was to be awarded the Military Medal. He was aged 22 and is buried at Etaples Military Cemetery in the Pas de Calais, France.

Chapter 2:
The Old End

Back-to-Backs and Tenements

If you stand facing the front of the Hip, the Hippodrome, in Hurst Street and look to your left, amidst all the newness of Brum's theatre quarter there are a few old buildings, now refurbished, on the corner of Hurst Street and Inge Street. These form the last back-to-backs in Birmingham. It is difficult to believe that there are so few left. In the 1930s there were over 40,000 of these dwellings in Birmingham. Built in terraces, they literally shared their back wall with another house behind that was part of yet another terrace. With no back door and no back windows, these small houses were dark and cramped – having as they did but one room downstairs, often with a tiny scullery above the cellar head.

Depending upon whether the back-to-back was of the two-storeys type or attic high (three storeys), there would either be two small bedrooms on the one level upstairs or a bedroom above which was an attic. All the facilities that we take for granted today as essential for our privacy were lacking. Most back-to-backs either ran up a yard and if not and they fronted on to the street, then they would share the yard at the rear. In this yard would be communal lavatories, miskins for rubbish, a brewus for washing and – until the 1930s – shared water taps.

During the inter-way years 200,000 Brummies lived in back-to-backs, equivalent to a city the size of Bolton, and as late as the 1960s tens of thousands of English, Irish, Scottish, Welsh, Jewish and Black Brummies made the best of things with homes that were outdated, decaying and inadequate. These Brummies were as responsible for making Birmingham the greatest manufacturing city in the world as were any other Brummies and yet there until recently there was no place that showed their lives and their impact upon history. Thankfully that major omission was addressed with the Court No. 15 Back to Backs Project of the Birmingham Conservation Trust and the National Trust.

I was a member of the Advisory Board of that project that aimed to transform the last back-to-backs in Hurst Street and Inge Street into a living museum, and I found inspiration for what we could do in Birmingham to honour working people in the Tenement Museum in New York. I went to New York in 2002 with a party of West Midlands firefighters to take part in the commemorations for the first anniversary of the terrible terrorist attack on the twin towers on 11 September 2001. We had been invited by firefighters from the Vinegar Hill Firehouse in Harlem, four of whom had visited Birmingham in March 2002 to lead our Saint Patrick's Parade.

As I was in New York, I was keen to see the Lower East Side Tenement Museum at 97, Orchard Street. In particular, I wanted to see how New Yorkers have approached the task of bringing to the fore the lives of those who have been hidden from history for too long. Crucially, the Lower East Side of Manhattan Island was the entry point to the New World for generations of immigrants and tenement living was much more the typical American experience than was the frontier.

The Tenement Museum itself is five stories high and it contained twenty apartments of three small rooms – all of which were approached via a shared and unlit hallway that was a fire hazard. Inside rooms had no access to air or light and homes were lit by candles or kerosene. Water was drawn from a tap in the back yard, where slops and garbage were emptied. Things improved in the early twentieth century as windows were added, gas was laid on and flushable toilets were installed between every two families. Still – and despite the different type of housing – the similarity with the living conditions of back-to-back Brummies is striking.

The Lower East Side Tenement Museum tells the stories of New York's immigrants powerfully and thoughtfully through showing the lives of certain families at various stages in the life of the tenement and via outstanding tours led by New Yorkers who know and care for the people who lived in these tenements. That example affected the deliberations of the Advisory Committee for the proposed Back to Back Museum in Birmingham, that people are now able to visit.

The long-awaited opening by the National Trust of the Inge Street back-to-backs close to the Hippodrome made the week beginning 19 July 2004 a momentous one for the history of Birmingham and most importantly for the history of working-class Brummies. At last the lives of those who had so often been hidden from sight in the investigation of the past are now brought into the full light of our awareness and appreciation.

It was a long campaign to save these houses in the heart of what is now Birmingham's theatre quarter. Back in the late 1980s I pressed for the saving of ten back-to-backs in Floodgate Street, Deritend, close to the corner with Fazeley Street. The front houses numbered 59-63 and there was a biggish yard to the rear, and I believed that

Carl outside 97, Orchard Street, the New York Tenement Museum in the Lower East Side.

these would make a fitting museum to bring to the fore the contribution of working-class folk to the making of Birmingham.

Lots of Brummies supported me, for which I am grateful, believing as I did that those hundreds of thousands of Brummies who had lived in back-to-backs ought to be remembered and honoured. They had endured hard lives, collaring for little reward and having to contend with high death rates, industrial diseases and pollution from the factories all around. Living in cramped conditions in small and often badly-built houses, they had carried on as best they could with little privacy, having to share communal brew'uses, miskins, lavatories, suffs, and cold water taps in the yard.

Despite this, the Brummies whose address was back of were a proud people. The vast majority of mothers strove daily to keep their families clean and respectable, and throughout back street Brummagem the ties of kinship and neighbourliness were vital features. These bonds allowed poorer people to fight back against their common enemy, poverty, and to create thriving neighbourhoods in which old ladies could pop out for a stick of ale in the dark nights with no worry of muggings, in which young wenches could walk the street safely and in which a babby who was clammed would be given a piece.

Unfortunately, those houses in Floodgate Street were in a ruinous condition and there was no chance of saving them. Eventually they were knocked down and with little official concern in highlighting working-class life, those of us determined not to let the lives of back-to-back Brummies be swept from history switched our attention to the houses on the corner of Inge Street and Hurst Street.

For several years the officers in the City's Planning Department, Conservation section and Museums showed their interest in the concept of restoring these back-to-backs and opening them up to the public. However, this objective could not have been achieved if it had not been for the backing of crucial figures. Amongst them was Derek Lea of James and Lister, who administered the Gooch Estate, upon whose land the back-to-backs stood. Derek

Court number 7 at the back of 33 or 34 Cheapside, about 1905. Thanks to Birmingham Library Services. Notice the standpipe in the yard, providing water for the families, and the ramshackle lavatories on the left. There is a man standing in the doorway of the house on the left.

Folk in a yard in Summer Lane in the 1920s. Notice the line full of clean washing.

and his colleague Charles Gillett were crucial – as were the Gooch family. Another key player was Councillor Mike Olley who brought in Les Sparks, Tony Davison and Toni Demidowicz of the City's Department of Planning and Architecture, and also the Birmingham Conservation Trust. There is no doubt that without the expertise of first Debbie Dance and then Elizabeth Perkins of the Trust that we would not have the back-to-backs now open to the public. Their work was supported strongly by Councillors David Roy and Renee Spector. Since then both English Heritage and the National Trust have made invaluable contributions.

Thankfully, the Birmingham Conservation Trust is working on another major project, the Newman Coffin Factory on the edge of the Jewellery Quarter. The task of saving our historic buildings and remembering those who went before has no ending. Let us all fight to ensure that we know where we come from – for if we lose our collective memory of the past, how can we understand the present or move confidently and alertly into the future? What is more how can our young people respect themselves and others if they do not know who they are and whence they come?

Five or Six? Five Ways

For the Brummies of the 1820s, Five Ways seemed to be at the end of the known world - a feeling made more strong by the fact that there were no street lamps past this place. At any rate, it was definitely at the outermost limits of their town, lying as it did at the south-western edge of the ancient manor of Birmingham. Beyond it were the fields of the rural parish of Edgbaston, through which Hagley Row took you to Halesowen. The Row itself was misnamed for it was not a straight road as was implied by its title. Instead, between the present Francis and Highfield Roads it curved noticeably towards the left. Even after the road was straightened, the existence of that bend was evident from the laid-back position of the old houses in that location.

Indeed, the newly rectilinear Hagley Road still appeared as a country lane, for on its left-hand side it was accompanied by a wide open ditch which usually was filled with dirty water and across which were bridges which allowed residents to reach their houses. Not that there were many buildings in the 1820s. Standing at Five Ways you could see the 'Plough and Harrow', then an old-fashioned pub, and that was about it. Further on, Chad House was another public house and there were perhaps half a dozen houses in its vicinity.

It's ten past four in the afternoon at Five Ways in the Edwardian era. Notice the horse drawn tram and the children by the statue of Joseph Sturge on the left, near to Ladywood Road, and facing down Broad Street. This is from a postcard given to me by Mr A. Vince of Mitcham, Surrey. It was posted on August 22 1908 at 10.30 in the morning and was sent to a Mrs Starkey in Addison Road, Kings Heath by Lil. The message read, 'If you come tonight and go up to May's first & I will leave a message there for you. In haste Lill'.

On the Birmingham side of Five Ways, development was a little more obvious. Broad Street was lined with private dwellings, each of which boasted a front garden, and it was dominated by the grand Bingley House, the home of the banking Lloyds. The street ended at Sheepcote Lane, and thence onwards it was called Islington - the same name as a neighbourhood which was in the throes of development on an estate which had been owned by Saint Martin's Church. This glebe land was cut through with the aptly-named Saint Martin's Street and Bishopsgate Street.

Mentioned in an abstract of title of premises between 1770-1822, Five Ways itself was the meeting place not only of Islington and Hagley Row but also of Islington Row, going in an easterly direction down the hill towards Bristol Street; of Long Lane to the south, which was the route to Harborne; and of Ladywood Lane on the west which meandered to Rotton Park and Smethwick.

These five ways had been running into each other from at least the 1600s, but in the 1820s they were joined by a sixth - Calthorpe Street. Taking its name from the family which still owns Edgbaston, it was soon filled with new houses and became the focus of an upmarket, middle-class district which from 1838 was served by the parish church of Saint George's. In that year, Edgbaston became part of Birmingham - but then as now Five Ways retained its old name despite the fact that it had become the junction of six ways. And over the next decade or so, Five Ways ceased to be on the margins of Brum and instead was changed into bustling landmark in a rapidly growing industrial town.

To the east, landowners such as Rylands and the governors of the King Edward's Trust ensured that Ladywood was transformed into a populous working-class area; and to the west, Edgbaston gained more and more residents as wealthy Brummies fled upwind from the smoke and smells of Brum into a more salubrious environment.

These developments turned Five Ways into a busy junction, noted for its policemen on point duty, its grammar school, its clock and its statue of a Quaker businessman called Joseph Sturgen who strove for the rights of Black and working-class people. Placed on a pedestal, it was inscribed with the words: 'He laboured to bring freedom to the Negro slave, the vote to British workmen, and the promise of peace to a war-torn world'. Sculpted in marble by John Thomas, the base of the statue had basins from which water rose up. On pedestals on either side were two life-size figures representing Sturge's beliefs: one was a woman depicting 'charity', nursing a child in her arms and giving food to a black youngster; whilst the other signifying 'Peace', was placed by a lamb, a dove and other peaceful symbols.

Under each was a drinking fountain, out of which water came via lilies before falling into marble shells. Sturge rose above these figures, one hand on the Bible and the other held out in a gesture of peace. The statue was placed in 1862 at Five Ways as it was the entrance to Edgbaston where Sturge lived. Its unveiling ceremony was attended by John Bright and William Scholefield, Birmingham's two MP's at the time, and over 12,000 people.

Today Five Ways is dominated by swirling traffic, a great roundabout and towering blocks of offices. The coppers have gone and so has the school. But at least the clock and Sturge's statue remain.

BROAD ST. FIVE WAYS B.HAM.

Looking down Broad Street from Five Ways in the 1930s.

In the late 1950s and early 1960s, Carol Penver worked for Midland Catering at Five Ways House - a large white building which now is a little more grey. Carol was in the restaurant where meals were made for the staff. She had to open up at 6.45 each morning and create the sweets for the lunchtime - 'with a variety of at least seven each day and with just one person helping me'. Amongst the sweets were apple tarts, roly poly, fresh fruit salad, ice cream and rice pudding made with prunes. The cooks also made pastry for Cornish pasties and meat pies for dinners and 'we worked hard'.

When Jean Smith was growing up in Bishopsgate Street, Five Ways was the playground for the local kids. Amongst the shops were Sibley's, which 'I think was a gentleman's outfitters but I could be wrong, and Salamis, the only Greek restaurant I had ever seen as a child. Then there was Bowkett's with their mouth-watering cakes and buns and if you bought 12 at a penny each you could have a baker's dozen, 13. They were still warm from the oven, smelling so delicious and topped with either chocolate or white icing. They also had Viennese whirls, coconut pyramids, macaroon tarts, shells, tarts filled with jam, lemon curd or treacle and many others - as well as fresh bread such as cottage loaves, tin loaves, brick torpedoes, batches, malt loaves and many more.'

On an evening, Jean and her pals used to play in the doorway of Boot's. This place was 'quite large and had a glass-tiled ceiling. We used to dance and watch ourselves in this. A little further along we would look in the windows of Hedge's the chemist and further along still was another chemist called Chase's and in their window were some very large glass containers. One was filled with what looked like peeled oranges and the other with oranges that looked like they had been cut in half and preserved.'

Gwen Rogers lived across Broad Street in Ladywood Road, having arrived in Brum from Nottingham in 1944 after meeting her Brummie husband whilst she was in the Land Army and he was in the RAF. Together with their 18 month old daughter they lived in at the top of the yard which was just down from then modern Tesco store at

Five Ways. They had a tiny house which was called the cottage. It was a shock to Gwen as she had never before seen a back-to-back house.

Times were hard and Gwen recalls that her chap would often walk to work to save the penny tramfare, whilst she would take thrupence 'for some pork bones from Baxter's on Broad Street and a penny worth of mixed veg.' That would make a dinner for four days. Later, Gwen got a part-time job at Kunzle's factory at Five Ways where 'we could buy damaged cakes. What a treat!'

June Wilson was born at 265 Hagley Road and went school at Edgbaston High, which then was on that road and near to Five Ways. In fact, June has always lived within walking distance of Five Ways and at one time had a flat overlooking the underpass. June's mother, Millicent, who owned Birmingham's only haute couture shop in New Street, and her uncle was Oscar Deutsch, who founded the Odeon chain of cinemas and who lived close to Five Ways.

One of her outstanding memories is of eating the delicious strawberry boats and fruit cake in Kunzle's shop and cafe. At the end of school terms, 'we Edgbaston High School Girls went to Kunzle's cafe for ice creams - we were daring enough to take or school hats off!' Almost opposite the school itself was Simpson's fish shop and Pattison's cafe. Also noticeable was Faulkes the furriers on Islington Row, outside of which there was a full-sized bear and other stuffed animals: 'these used to frighten me to death as a child! Nor has June forgotten Barrow's Stores, the Maypole Dairies and the Home and Colonial.

This was the day in which the 'one way traffic system' came into operation on Five Ways. Usually one of the busiest points in the city 'it was deserted this morning owing to the rapid clearance of traffic'. But what's the date? The policeman is standing close to Calthorpe Road and is looking down Islington Row. The other policeman is standing on the end of Broad Street.

Where is it? Perry Barr

Where is Perry Barr? To nearly all Brummies that would seem a foolish question, and we would answer quickly – 'It's by the "Crown and Cushion, on the big island along the Birchfield Road'. But in fact what most of us think of as Perry Barr is actually Birchfield – with Perry Barr itself beginning beyond the 'One Stop Shopping Centre' and across the River Tame. The emergence of the name Perry Barr south of the Tame arose because of the local railway station. In 1837 the Grand Junction Railway began running trains between Birmingham and Liverpool. One of the earliest stations on the line was opened in Birchfield in 1837 but for some reason it was called Perry Barr Station. Consequently, as the surrounding neighbourhood grew it became known as part of Perry Barr.

Historically, Perry Barr proper lay in the parish of Handsworth – with the manor of Perry being the land to the north east of the River Tame. Later this area would form a separate township to that of Handsworth. The place name itself is made up of two old names: Perry, from the Old English word 'pirige' meaning pear tree, and the Celtic word 'barr' signifying hill top.

At the time of the Domesday Book in 1086 the locality was simply Perry and was held by Drew from the powerful lord of Dudley, William FitzAnsculf. It was assessed at three hides, possessed a mill and its population consisted of three villeins and three

A wonderful shot of a rural Rocky Lane, Perry Barr in the very early twentieth century.

bordars and their families. Before the Conquest it had been held by Leofwaru. It is likely that he was one of the many Anglo-Saxon thegns whose land was taken from them by the Normans.

The history of the ownership of Perry Manor is complicated. Still by the mid-sixteenth century, half of it was held of it by the Wyrley family - members of whom were prominent in the district as far back as the thirteenth century. Through them it descended with the manor of Handsworth to the Birch family. In 1848, this portion of the lordship was bought by the Goughs, who had purchased the other half of the manor in 1669. Thus united, Perry came under the sway of the same family which owned Edgbaston.

Its manor house, Perry Hall, stood on the banks of the River Tame at the bottom of the present Perry Avenue. In the early twentieth century it was the home of General S.J. Gough, who later became the seventh Baron Calthorpe. The hall had been knocked down by the early 1930s, by which time much of its estate had been bought by the City for Perry Hall Playing Fields. The Home Farm of the lords of the manor lay to the south of the hall and close to the future Perry Barr Dog Track. The Cliveden Road Estate of private houses now occupies the land.

For a time in the later Middle Ages, there was a manor of Parva (Little) Barr. Indeed, the Domesday Book gives two entries for Barr: one has the same tenant as Aldridge and probably was Great Barr; the other was held by Drew, and given that a man with same name held Perry, it is likely that this second Barr was Little Barr.

It is likely that this smaller Barr adjoined Perry, and from an early date they were deeply connected with each other. In 1327 the taxpayers of the two manors were listed together; whilst by the end of that century they were held jointly. By the early fifteenth century Little Barr appears to have become part of Perry.

However, its former separate existence led to a name change for Perry. By the later eighteenth century, the place was

Perry Hall. A Tudor mansion, it had been visited in 1885 by Edward, The Prince of Wales – later to be Edward VII. It was demolished in the early twentieth century despite protests that such an act would be vandalism.

known as Perry Barr, Pury Barr, or Parva Barr. As a result, the name Perry came to be used only for the small village just across the Perry Bridge and around the church of Saint John the Evangelist in Church Road. This place of worship was consecrated in 1833 and became a separate parish from Handsworth in 1862.

Thirty-two years later the separate existence of Perry Barr was confirmed when it became an urban district. But as with King's Norton to the south of Birmingham, urban was something of a misnomer - for in 1921 Perry Barr had just 2,700 people and its gas and water was supplied from Birmingham. Seven years later the authority was extinguished when it was divided between West Bromwich and Birmingham. The City gained three quarters of the land but less than half of its people. But with the development of Kingstanding, Perry Barr's population increased rapidly and greatly to 20,214 by 1931. Twenty years later, following the urbanisation of the rest of the district, it had swollen to 76,391.

By this date a number of areas had emerged within Perry Barr. They included Kingstanding, of course, Hamstead, Oscott, Perry Common, and Tower Hill - where private housing was built on the land of Tower Hill Farm. At the same time, much of the northern part of the district had come to be called Great Barr. For most of its history Great Barr was part of the parish of Aldridge in Staffordshire. Some of it is now in Walsall, but much of it has been absorbed into West Bromwich. Great Barr, then, is outside Birmingham. Yet many people refer to the Booth's Farm Estate in

Building work in Perry Barr in the 1950s.

Birmingham as Great Barr, which actually begins beyond the 'Scott Arms'; and it is also known as Perry Beeches because it was the site of Perry Wood.

Early in the nineteenth century, William Booth was a notorious forger and minter of false coins. On 28 March 1812 the military attacked the fortified Booth's Farm and when he was captured the authorities found £3,000 in good notes, 200 guineas in gold, £600 in counterfeit silver coins and a large amount of forged notes. Booth was sent for trial at Stratford Assizes. Four years previously he had been tried at Warwick for the murder of his brother, John, but had been acquitted for lack of evidence.

This time he was not so fortunate. Booth was executed publicly on 15 August 1815, but the hangman bungled the job and so the false coiner had to be revived and hanged again two hours later. He was buried at Handsworth Old Church and later moved. Thus, Booth was tried twice, hanged twice and buried twice.

To the east of the Booth's Farm Estate, the name Great Barr has also come into use on the former land of Brooklyn Farm. This has resulted from the presence of Great Barr School on the Aldridge Road. The greater part of both districts was developed from the inter-war years with private and council housing. One of the last rural outposts to disappear in Perry Barr was Blakelands Farm. Lying to the west of the Kingstanding Road and to the north of the canal, it was under cultivation in the early 1950s. It succumbed to development soon after and is now an estate of private housing.

If Perry Barr has lost its northern localities, it has gained in the south, across the River Tame, where it has taken in much of Birchfield - around the 'Crown and Cushion'. The Wellhead Lane neighbourhood here is of particular interest. Today it is dominated by the University of Central England, but in the late 1840s it was laid out as the first freehold land society estate in the Birmingham area. Such societies were in the forefront of the battle for working-class rights. Bonding together in freehold land societies, better-off working-class men could buy land more cheaply in the shires where it was easier to get the vote than in boroughs like Birmingham. Through their membership of a building society, such men then could build a house that gave them the vote.

In the case of the Wellhead Lane Estate, the men belonged to the Investment and Permanent Benefit Building Society. Possession was taken in May 1848 when members of the society marched in triumph from Birmingham. One of the roads cut out was the well-named Franchise Street. To the north of this development was Oldford Farm. Today its land is owned by the great Birmingham-based multinational firm, IMI.

Dominated today by Perry Park, the Alexander Sports Stadium and the Birmingham Crematorium, Perry Barr may no longer be as big as it was but it continues to make a strong impact on Birmingham.

The Right to Battle. Shard End

It was one of the most remarkable events in English legal history, the trial of Abraham Thornton of Shard End. In 1817 the unfortunate Mary Ashford was murdered after she had attended a hop at the 'Tyburn House' pub. 'A pretty country girl from Erdington', she had danced with Thornton and he was the last person to be seen with her later that night. Accused of the killing, Thornton was acquitted for lack of evidence but local people still believed in his guilt and Mary's younger brother, William, used an old and almost forgotten statute, Appeal of Murder, to bring Thornton to book. This allowed a close relative of the victim to demand another trial despite the acquittal of the defendant.

At the appeal, Thornton was asked whether he was guilty of the crime. His reply amazed those in the courtroom and the whole legal profession, harking back as it did to the Middle Ages and trial by combat. Defiantly, Thornton declared 'Not guilty and I am ready to defend the same with my body'. Claiming the Right to Battle, he drew a pair of leather gloves and threw one down at William Ashford, daring the young man to take up the gauntlet and fight him. Such an event had not occurred since 1638 and faced by a

Abraham Thornton's Farm, Shard End. Later known as Mitchell's Farm it was knocked down soon after this photo was taken in 1953 and replaced by the 'Harlequin' pub.

burlier and stronger man, William withdrew his charge. Soon after, both Appeal of Murder and Right by Battle were abolished and Thornton emigrated to America.

Thornton lived at what was known later as Mitchell's Farm and which became the site of the 'Harlequin' pub. He and his father were tenants of Lord Bradford, and at that time – as it had been for centuries – Shard End was part of Castle Bromwich.

Though until recently it was a little-populated rural spot, Shard End is not lacking in history. In the later nineteenth century a researcher called Christopher Chattock stated that an ancient but corroded spear had been found in two fields called Upper and Lower Britain Berrows. Be that as it may, the name berrow suggests a barrow, a mound of earth constructed in the period Before Christ to cover one or more burials.

Berrowside Road recalls these field names, however, the earliest documentary evidence for Shard End comes from the thirteenth century in a grant of land made by Thomas of le Scherd in Bromwic. Shard may derive from the Old English word 'sceard', a gap or pass in the Forest of Arden – but it is more likely that it comes from the Middle English 'sherd', a detached and isolated part of a manor. Thus, Shard End was a remote part at one of the ends of the manor of Castle Bromwich.

Shard End Carnival in the late 1950s. Does anyone recognise a face and have memories of the event?

For centuries Shard End remained remote, with farms such as Shard End Farm in the area of All Saints Church and rural meanderings like Popit Lane, now part of Shard End Crescent. Then there was wonderfully-named Maggoty Lane, now Bucklands End Lane, whilst Buckland End and part of the Heath Way were called Black Mire Lane. Also part of Castle Bromwich and bound with Shard End, Buckland End was known originally as Bockenholt, - the beech (bocken) wood (holt), and is mentioned as such in the thirteenth century.

Along with Hodge Hill, both Bucklands End and Shard End were taken from Castle Bromwich in 1931 and brought into Birmingham. Fourteen years later, soon after peace came to Europe, plans were put forward to compulsory purchase the farmland locally and develop it as a council estate. Shard End itself became the single biggest corporation estate in the city with a total of 3,870 houses.

In particular, folk from Duddeston, Nechells, Ashted, Vauxhall and Saltley were moved to the new area – but the rural past of Shard End has not been forgotten for the area boasts one of the most active and important local history societies in the City.

A cracking photo of shops on the new Shard Estate in 1955. Thanks to the Birmingham Evening Mail. Alf W. Beck recalls that these shops were in the same spot as are the present shops in Shard End Crescent 'except that you can see that they were single storey and were faced the reverse of the present ones. Access to the shops was by a small court off Shustoke Road where the library now stands.'

In the early 1950s these were the only shops near to where Alf lived in Brook Meadow Road. There were no buses going that way and folk had to walk up to a mile to fetch their shopping. There were some traders who came around in small vans and sold groceries out of the back and 'Sunday papers were bought off a man who had a cart and sold his wares on the corner of Cole Hall Lane and Bucklands End'.

In those early days of Shard End estate there was no church and Dr Mayberry's surgery was two small houses/flats on the corner of Brownfields Way and the Heathway. Nor were there any schools locally and each day Alf's eleven year old son was taken by bus to Perry Common. Eventually schools were built, but Alf remains astonished that two of them, Alderlea Boys and Longmeadow Girls have since been demolished.

Mrs F. Pullen moved to Timberley Lane 53 years ago and recalls that on Coronation Day the celebrations were held in the old farm building that had belonged to the Mitchells. The prefabricated shops themselves 'were a boon to all of us who eventually came to live in the area, the biggest being the Co-op. Also we had a Post Office inside a sweet shop run by Miss Keen and she was a real one for discipline. When the proper shops were built almost everyone from the prefab shops moved as well. I also took my sons for the opening by the Queen of All Saints Church and one of my sons married there and both his daughters were christened there.'

Joan Eden notes that there was no proper road laid between the shops 'and it had the appearance of a cowboy town: dusty when it was warm and muddy when it was wet; however there was a good variety of shops. I moved into a new flat in Kitsland Road in February 1958. There were six blocks, all with Australian names. To me it was like winning the lottery. Rents were £2 12s and 10 pence, which included heating and hot water. The outsides of the blocks were kept immaculate by the caretakers and the neighbours were the best! These beautiful flats are now being demolished too.'

Eileen Jobson tells me that although the shops were built as a temporary measure for the new estate – as Shard End then was – they lasted many years. Around the corner from them, All Saints Church was also just a hut in those days. Eileen also makes another and most important point. In all the publicity about the recently refurbished back-to-backs in Inge Street, too often the houses have been described as slums. Eileen and many others who have contacted me have rightly been upset by this description. Eileen lived in Irving Street until she was twelve 'and those houses were spotless. Every morning the steps, windowsills and outside were washed. We shared a toilet but they were clean. We took pride in our homes. In our backyard and many others we took pride in our little back houses. We didn't have much but we were not slums.'

Macca's Estate to Sheldon

Throughout modern Birmingham, long-dead Anglo-Saxons call out to us that they live on through the place names we use daily and take for granted. There's Dudda who had an estate (ton) that is recalled in Duddeston, one of the oldest recorded place names in Birmingham for it is mentioned as Duddestone in a deed of King Ethelred dated 963 and then appears in the Curia Regia Rolls of 1204 as Dodeston. Then there's Bordesley, which may mean the clearing in the wood made by a man called Bord, or perhaps the clearing where boards were got. And Billesley. An area of light sand and gravel that lay in the parish and manor of Yardley, Worcestershire, Billesley means Bill's clearing in the wood.

It is likely that the name emerged before the Norman Conquest of 1066 and that Bill and his family were like other settlers in the Forest of Arden in the late Anglo-Saxon period – they struck out from the main village to make a home in a distant and isolated part of a manor. In Chelmsley Wood, Ceolmund Crescent reminds us of another Anglo-Saxon. The area was first mentioned around 1200 as the wood called Chelemundesheia and it means the wood of someone called Ceolmund.

Similarly, Edgbaston brings to mind a chap named Ecbald and his estate (tun), Cotteridge may mean the ridge of Cotta; and Erdington signifies the estate of Earda. To their number can be added Frankley, the clearing of Franca; Handsworth, the enclosure or enclosed settlement (worth) of a man called Hun; Oscott, a cott (cottage) of a fellow named Osa; and Mackadown Lane. This latter is derived from Machintone, which was entered into the Domesday Book of 1086. It signifies the estate of Macca and is recalled in Mackadown Lane.

Mackadown Farm, which stood at the junction of Mackadown Lane and Tile Cross Road, was probably laid out by Macca sometime between 800 and 1000 AD. He chose carefully, because the farm was a place where the soil of sand and gravel was lighter than the rest of the locality, which was made up of heavy clay covered by woods. As such it was easier to clear of trees and to farm. The Anglo-Saxon settlers of Yardley chose the same kind of spot, cultivating their fields on a sand patch to the north of the old village and its church.

Given as Makinton in a document of 1220, Mackadown had water meadows to its east and south, close to Kingshurst Brook and Platt Brook – across from which was Radley Moor. To the north of the settlement the land was cleared for two, small open fields: Elder and Rye-Eddish. Later another emerged – Ridding, which itself means clearing. Rye-Eddish Field lay in the middle and had a trackway either side. Their lines are followed today by Mackadown Lane and Tile Cross Road. The outlying land gave common pasture, and importantly there was a fresh water spring nearby.

In the Domesday Book of 1086, there was no mention of Sheldon. Instead an entry was made for Machintone. That monumental gathering of information about England ordered by William the Conqueror showed that fourteen peasant men lived on the manor, perhaps giving a population of about 60, and that it was worth 40 shillings.

This was about fifteen more people than the manor of Birmingham, of course a much smaller place then, which was valued at half the amount.

Machintone was owned by Turchill, an intriguing figure. He was one of the few Anglo-Saxon thegns, a person of high rank, who kept his lands following the Norman Conquest. Most of his properties were in the Forest of Arden. Indeed, he owned 67 out of the 297 Domesday manors in Warwickshire. Unsurprisingly, by 1088 he was calling himself Turchill de Arden and it is likely that he was an ancestor of Mary Arden, Shakespeare's mother. Turchill's descendants, continued to own significant estates, amongst them Park Hall in Castle Bromwich, Peddimore in Sutton Coldfield, Saltley and Berwood (now Castle Vale).

Machintone was held from Turchill by another Anglo-Saxon, Alnod. It is probable that he lived in his hall in the village and that he had strips amongst the open fields with the other villagers. The next recorded tenant in 1220 brought into view the name Sheldon, for he was Ansel de Scheldon. Described as the lord of the manor of Makintone, Ansel's descendants held the manor for over the next one hundred years. It is likely that they lived at what became Sheldon Hall. This lay to the north of the original settlement and was the centre of the lord's demesne, his home farm.

A deed of 1570 indicated that Sheldon Hall was bounded to the east by the land of Henry Casemore, which became known as Cashmoor's Meadow; to the north by the River Cole; and to the west by Outmoor, recalled later in Outmoor Farm and today in Outmoor Road. It was on this western edge of the demesne that stood Babbs Mill. It is probable that this was owned directly by the lord, and in the Middle Ages all of the people of his manor had to bring their corn to be ground.

The lord's estate also seemed to include two portions of land detached from the home farm. These were Hardwick and Berwick, both of which mean outlying lands of the manor and both of which were located on the northern edges of two of the ancient fields of Machintone – Rye-Eddish and Ridding.

In his pioneering work on 'Discovering Sheldon', Victor Skipp suggested that the 60 folk of the manor would have been unable to produce enough to live on from these two fields and the other long-cultivated field, Elder. Accordingly, even before the Norman Conquest the villagers would have moved out beyond the common pastures of Kitts Green and Garretts Green to clear the abundant oak trees locally and form new fields on the heavier lands of clay. These fields were Holifast, Ashole, Beriots, Monland, Ashforlonge and Cockshutt – brought to mind now by Cockshutt Hill.

With the marked growth in population in England in the twelfth and thirteenth centuries, further agricultural expansion was needed. For this the folk of Machintone looked south across the Plant Brook and the black, peaty soil of Radley Moor – remembered in The Radleys - and then across Kingshurst Brook to another area of clay soils. The new fields cultivated were Great Sheldon, Greatock and Hatchford, leading to Hatchford Brook, whilst there was common land in Upper Radley Moor, Outwoods and Wells Green. Remote from Machintone, they necessitated a new settlement called Sheldon, named after the lords of the manor.

Mott House was an eighteenth-century building of red brick and was demolished in 1960. Its moat was supplied by water from Kingshurst Brook, once called Easthall Brook. Of the other two manor houses of Sheldon, Kent's moat is now just a ditch, bank and open space; whilst Sheldon Hall is now a pub and restaurant.

In 1939 Mott House was described as the only moated farm house in Birmingham: a 'picturesque old place in Sheldon it will shortly be knocked down for a modern housing estate'. June Mears told me that the photo showed Moat Farm. June herself moved into Sheldon Grove, right on the edge of the Moat, in 1958. This was part of the Cranespark Estate and her home was one of those built by Dare's, the famous Birmingham building firm that was also prominent in the development of much of Hall Green.

June and her family moved in when the farm still stood. In it lived two ladies called Mary and Rose, who belonged to two separate families, and the father of one of them. This man had been on the land but was now an invalid. When there was heavy rain, the kitchen in their cottage was flooded. June recalled that she spoke to the man who was in charge of the building site and he stated that the ground hereabouts was so soft because of the moat that the workers 'had to go down 22 feet for piledriving for the flats and nine feet under our houses'.

Kindly, June sent me an old newspaper cutting with another view of Moat Farm. The caption stated that 'the picturesque scene of the Moat farm at Sheldon, surrounded by trees and a moat, has now been replaced by housing'. The photo was sent in by a Mr Gerald Thompson of Solihull who said that the farmhouse was demolished and the moat filled in by 1960 and that the houses that replaced Moat Farm stood opposite Cranes Park Road. Even though it is no longer there, the modern A to Z still shows Moat House between Westley Brook Close, off Common Lane, and Church Road - opposite the start of Cranespark Road and by the Roman Catholic Church and school of Saint Thomas More.

62   *Brum and Brummies: Volume 4*

It was successful and by 1330 the nave and chancel of Saint Giles, Sheldon had been put up. Indeed, so successful was the new village that the name of Sheldon came to dominate over that of Machintone. By the late 1300s, Sheldon Manor had been divided into three; the East Hall based on Sheldon Hall; the West Hall, thought to be at Kent's Moat; and Lyndon Manor focused on Mott House, which stretched into Bickenhill.

In the Middle Ages, agriculture was based on great open fields which were divided into strips. The better off had the most strips and the poorest had none. However, some people struck out on their own and made their own clearances with the permission of the lord of the manor. These small, hedged fields were enclosed and the wider community had no rights to them. As time went on, the more prosperous villagers decided that they did not want their land spread out in strips in open fields. They sought to bring their holdings together and enclose them, to make them separate from the other villagers and so make it easier for them to cultivate. This process was achieved slowly by exchanging some strips and buying others.

Enclosure like this gradually led to the loss of Cockshut Field and others, but as late as 1706 the three ancient fields of Machintone and the three of Sheldon remained open. A Tithe Account for 1706 records that Sheldon Field was fallow and that Greatock and Hatchford Fields were stripped. The same was true of Elder, Rye-Eddish and Ridding fields in Machintone.

Lyndon Manor was the third manor in Sheldon. Its manor house of Moat Farm or the Mott House lay a few hundreds south west of the parish church of Saint Giles. The manor also had property in Church Bickenhill nearby but it was focused on the three open fields of Great Sheldon, Greatock and Hatchford. During the eighteenth century they were enclosed and in his pioneering work on Sheldon, Victor Skipp showed in detail how this happened in Yew Furlong of Greatock Field, which gave its name to Greatock Lane – now called Cranes Park Road.

Once the better-off landowners had swapped strips with each other to gather their strips in one field, they then sought to bring their strips together. In 1706 the Allen family owned most of the strips in the north, Mott House most of those in the centre, and John and Phil Wells most of those in the south. By 1840 the strips of Yew Furlong had disappeared. They had been replaced by three enclosed fields: in the north, New Inclosure was held by Richard Farmer, who had succeeded the Allens; in the south, Yew Furlong was farmed by John Wells; and in the centre, Great Oak Field belonged to Charles Nossiter who farmed from the Mott House.

In 1813, the commons and wastes of Sheldon were also enclosed. These included Outmoor Green, Kitt's Green, Garrett's Green, Radley Moor, Outwoods, Gortys Pleck and Wells Green. The commons were essential for the survival of the poor, allowing them to rear an animal and have some rights and independence locally. But the rich resented the few and fragile rights of the poor and overturned them by enclosure. Nothing was left for the poor. It was a move that led to tension and disturbances in many parts of the country, although not as it seems in Sheldon. Local folk were given a share of the commons according to the size of their holdings. This meant that the lord of the manor, Earl Digby, took the most – over 50 acres. Cottagers had as little as a perch. That was just five yards, one foot and six inches, and was nowhere near enough to live on.

By this date, the farmers of Sheldon had begun to move away from rearing cattle for sale and growing corn for subsistence. Now wheat, rye, barley, oats and peas were the most important aspects of agriculture, with pigs, cows and sheep subsidiary. Enclosure and the development of better farming methods allowed Sheldon to become a corn-growing parish. This in turn led to the emergence of a small group of families with the most land.

In the early 1700s, almost every family in Sheldon had something to call their own, but by 1840 there had been a radical change. The number of farms paying the corn tithe, a tax to the parish church, had dropped drastically from 55 to 20 - and they farmed about 2,400 acres out of the total of 2,500. All bar three of these big farmers were newcomers. The old Sheldon families had either moved away to look for a better life, become agricultural labourers or paupers. By contrast, as powerful as any Medieval lord were the Digbys, who owned 75% of Sheldon.

Between 1841 and 1921, Sheldon's population hovered between 400 and 500 and it remained a deeply rural place. Its farms included Outmoor, demolished in 1950; Tile Cross, knocked down two years later; Bell, cleared in 1957; Malthouse, demolished in the early 1950s; Mackadown and Hullery, both fetched down before 1950; and Lower Barn Farm which became Hatchford Brook Golf Course. Sheldon's five inns have fared better. The Wheatsheaf, The Three Horse Shoes and The Bell are now modern pubs with old names; The White Hart, which although having some alterations still has much of its original building; and The Ring o' Bells. This stood opposite the parish church of Saint Giles and is now a pair of cottages.

Sheldon also had two windmills, one of which was Sheldon Mill. This stood on high ground to the south of the church and overlooked the Coventry Road. In addition there were three watermills, two of which are only known about through fields called Mill meadow. The other was Babb's Mill, which may have been on the site of the original manorial mill. Standing south of the Cole, it was certainly there in the eighteenth century and in 1751 it was taken over from Edward Cook of Sheldon by John Barrs, a baker of Yardley. It was still grinding corn in 1889, but by 1961 the pool it had been converted into two cottages.

By this date, Sheldon had undergone remarkable change. It had become a populous suburb of Birmingham. As far from city centre as any other district apart from Northfield and Longbridge, most of Sheldon became part of Birmingham in 1931, along with Wells Green. This was that part of Solihull which lay to the north of the Coventry Road and between Horse Shoe Lane and Sheaf Lane. Sheldon included Garrett's Green and Tile Cross and its total population was just 526 - only 103 more than it had been in 1821.

Sylvia Grundy, nee Mather, grew up in Cranes Park Road, Sheldon and this photo shows residents from there and Forest Hill Road on a day trip in the late 1940s. On the front row left to right are: Shirley Moore, Pat Weatherall, Maureen Hemming, Sylvia herself, Shirley's sister Marion with the bucket and spade, and Pat's brother Tony with the bottle of pop. On the back row are Mrs Ward,

Sylvia's Mom, Annie Lines her Dad's sister, Mrs Hemming, Mrs Moore and Mrs Weatherall. As Sylvia observes, 'we always called everyone Mr and Mrs in those days so I don't know many of the first names of my friends parents'.

Forest Hill Road was Sylvia's playground 'as most of my friends lived there. I remember the winter of 1947 we had some fun with our sledges going down Forest Hill Road but when people put ashes down we thought they were spoil sports, but now I am older I can understand why they did it.

'We played all the old street games up there, Kingie, Queenie, kick the can, May I cross your golden river, Polly on the mopstick and many more. We used to walk a lot with our friends and we used to go to Marston Green down Cranes Park in to Park Dale Road, then down the gulley into the playing field along the River Cole, over by the golf links as we used to call them, through the fields to Marston Green Station and sometimes up to Chelmsley Wood to pick the blue bells. The playing fields are now Sheldon Country Park. It is still much the same round there and by the Church.

'The shops have changed a lot. Bottom of Cranes Park Road where it joins Church Road, the shops that were there when I lived there in the 40s and 50s were the chemist with the blue, green and purple bottles and a door at the back; then a drapers called Jones and Moseley; next a butcher's called Field's; and then Woodfield's, it was two shops, a sweet shop and a hardware shop. Next was a large greengrocer's called Hodreon's, then there was a Wrenson's and a hairdresser's. I can't remember the name. We all used the local shops in those days.

'The buses did not run along Cranes Park Road until after the war, just the trolley bus along the Coventry Road. The Midland Red ran along Church Road from Marston Green. It was only a single decker and it had to go down under the bridge and down to the Radleys.'

The only concentration of people was around the church of Saint Giles, although there were some houses along the Coventry Road, Sheaf Lane, Horse Shoes Lane and Common Lane, formerly Outwood Lane. By the end of the 1930s, this situation had been transformed. Private house builders developed the Wells Green and Sheldon village localities, the Cranes Park Estate was built up, whilst the council began to lay out the huge Kent's Moat Estate with 1,227 houses.

From the late 1940s, with the south and west of Sheldon mostly urbanized, building activity now moved north and eastward to the Radleys, Garrets Green, Tile Cross, Mackadown and Cooks Lane localities. Cooks Lane had been called Ford Lane, whilst Tile Cross was recorded as Tylecross on Beighton's Map of 1725. The name suggests that it was a place where tiles were made. Certainly, in nearby Yardley there were tilers in the early fifteenth century. However in one of the documents of the Sheldon Charities it is written as Tyler's Cross, indicating that it was named after someone called Tyler. This seems to be the more likely origin. Birmingham's first post-war flats were erected in Tile Cross Road.

As for Garretts Green Named it recalls a family of local landowners and it was known as such by the early 1600s. A small settlement was focused on what became the great circle upon which stands East Birmingham College. It was connected to Sheldon and The Lea (Lea Hall) by Sheldon Heath Road, originally Platt Lane; whilst Garrett's Green Lane, then called Flint Lane, ran west only so far as Cockshut Hill. Plans were laid for a council estate during the 1930s, but building did not start for another twenty years. The sweeping away of the countryside was heralded by the council's development of the Chestnut Estate on which 649 houses were erected. This was followed by the loss of Outmoor Farm. Further development locally came under the council's Kent's Moat Estate.

Despite these massive developments, Saint Giles' still looks as if it is a village church and with its country park, Sheldon retains much greenery. Above all, a few road names call out of the past. One of them is Brays Road. Thomas Bray was the rector of Sheldon and in 1696 he was assigned to help the youthful church in Maryland in the United States of America. To help him in his task, Bray started the Society for the Propagation of Christian Knowledge. In 1922 the Bishop of Birmingham was presented with the state flag of Maryland in recognition of Bray's achievements. It hangs in St Philips Cathedral.

I should like to pay tribute to the assiduous research of Victor Skipp in uncovering the history of Sheldon.

A portion of the land given for a King George V Memorial Park at Sheldon, showing the parish church of Saint Giles in the background, in 1936. Thanks to the Birmingham Evening Mail.

Roy Roberts was born in September 1937 and is the eldest of three children. As a youngster he brings to mind that 'my brother and I were living with Mom and Dad in a back to back in Cattell Road, Small Heath. On the outbreak of war Dad was conscripted into the Royal Navy and he was killed in action on the Aircraft Carrier HMS Glorious in June 1940, two weeks before his 22nd birthday. At this time my Mother was pregnant with my sister Gloria.

'A wonderful Aunt and Uncle, who in about 1935/36 had moved to Dovercourt Road on the Cranes Park Estate – and I believe in those days the purchase price was about £364 – because of Mom's circumstances took us all to live with them., and my sister was born shortly afterwards. My Aunt lost two sons shortly after giving birth to them and never had any more children but was devoted to us as we were to her.

'I had a wonderful childhood in Sheldon and do remember the moated farmhouse referred to in your second article. In the late 1940s until it was demolished in the early fifties it was derelict and me and my pals used to have a great time exploring around it. We used to roam for miles in those halcyon days, across the fields, through Marston Green Village and then through Chelmsley Woods or Bluebell Woods to us kids.

'Looking at the A-Z Map now, Sheldon Country Park, King George V Playing Fields, Hatchford Brook Golf Course and the now extended runway at Birmingham

Airport were all fields owned by farmer Bell, whose farm house and barns were where the golf course meets the runways. During the war years and just after some of the fields were used for grazing but most were used to sow crops rotationally and nothing was pinched to my knowledge, except for a few ears of corn as we strolled through.

'I loved school and attended Silvermere Road as an infant, junior and senior. Being so close to the airfield the school suffered some bomb damage to the first floor and round about 1943/44 I remember being taken with my class to see a plane which had crashed in the field opposite, narrowly missing the school. These fields opposite Silvermere School also belonged to Farmer Bell and are now where the Mapledene Estate and School have been built.

'Lastly, at last a mention of Saint Giles's Church, Sheldon, one of the oldest and most interesting in the region. They have been sealed up now, but I remember seeing "lepers" windows on the South Wall, and on the North Wall inside the church is a brass plaque giving all the names and dates of the rectors of the parish from I think 1368, including the famous Thomas Bray. I was in the choir from 1947-50 and was surprised to see a photograph of myself and other friends in the choir in the recently published *Around Sheldon* by Margaret D. Green. I am the tallish fair-haired lad centre of picture. What a shock.'

Waxing Lyrical about Old Vauxhall

There's scarce a heart that will not start,
No matter what its rank or station,
And heave a sigh when they destroy,
This favourite place of recreation.
If we look back on memory's track,
What joyous scenes we can recall,
Of happy hours in its gay bowers,
And friends we met at Old Vauxhall.

So lamented Edward Farmer in 1850 at the disappearance of one of the oldest and most famed pleasure gardens outside London, those at Vauxhall in Duddeston. Owned by the Holtes for centuries, Duddeston was the home manor of the wealthy landowning family until the building of Aston Hall in the early years of the seventeenth century. Even then some members remained at Duddeston Hall, the last of whom was Lady Ann Holte who probably lived there until she died in 1738.

Within a few years of her death, the grand building became the focal point of large-scale cock fights between the 'gentlemen' of Warwickshire and those of nearby counties. Large sums were wagered. On 28 February 1748, ironically and unhappily for such a cruel activity this was Easter Monday, three days of cockfighting began between the gentlemen of Herefordshire and Worcestershire on the one side and those of Warwickshire and Staffordshire on the other. Each party weighed 41 cocks for ten guineas a battle and 200 guineas the Main – the match. Bye battles for 21 cocks aside were held at five guineas a battle.

Cock fighting continued for some years, although Duddeston Hall itself was transformed into a public house and its grounds gradually became a place of gentle and not blood-thirsty amusement. In June 1758, Andrew Butler informed the people of Birmingham that 'Duddeston Hall, commonly called Vauxhall, near Birmingham in Warwickshire, is now fitted up in a neat and commodious Manner for the reception of Travellers', and that the garden for public entertainment continued as usual. Probably taking its name from the place in London, Vauxhall became a major attraction. In July 1777 its appeal was highlighted by musical entertainments that drew in a 'brilliant' gathering.

In particular, the Gardens were praised for their fine condition, 'the Beauty of which, added to the elegant Appearance of the Company, particularly the Ladies, the Serenity of the Evening, and the Admirable Performance of the Concert, diffused a Cheerfulness and Approbation over the Countenance of the Performers.' The popularity of Vauxhall as a place of entertainment and recreation, its rural location close to the River Rea, its tranquillity and its charm held an allure for Brummies that led them to wax lyrical. One such was the Poet Freeth, after whom a modern street is named.

Old Vauxhall Gardens drawn by E. H. New, from a picture owned by Sir Benjamin Stone and printed in Robert K. Dent, The Making of Birmingham, 1894.

Based at his tavern in the Bull Ring, close to where the Fish Market would be built in Bell Street, Freeth was renowned as a publican-cum-balladeer-cum-poet. His poem, 'An Invitation to Vauxhall, extols the 'sweet native bowers', the fresh air and peaceful amusements of the place.

When the evening is fine, how enlivening the Scene,
The walks to parade, or to trip o'er the green'
No troubles to harass, no fears to alarm,
The mid sits at ease when there's Music to charm;
Then quickly away, to the region's resort,
Which Pleasure makes choice of for keeping her Court.

Enchanting to all classes of Birmingham society, the only noise to disturb the calm of Vauxhall was the whoosh and bang of fireworks in celebrated pyrotechnic displays. With its gravel walks lined with trees, bowling green, orchestra and pyrotechnic displays, Vauxhall Gardens drew to its delights not only the wealthy of Birmingham but also its shopkeepers and working people. Its popularity was highlighted by a poem from Bissett's *Poetic Survey and Magnificent Directory* (1808):

A rural spot where tradesmen oft repair,
For relaxation and to breathe fresh air;
The beauties of the place prove
To those who quiet and retirement love;
There, freed from toils and labours of the day
Mechanics with their wives, or sweethearts, stray;
Or rosy children, sportive, trip along
To see rare Fireworks - or to hear a song
For oft in summer Music's sweet powr's
Woos thousands to Vauxhall to pass their hours.

As late as 1839, Vauxhall Gardens were described by John Alfred Langford as 'in their splendour', whilst galas were given frequently 'and singers of the first-class reputation were engaged'. By contrast, two years previously, Drake in *The Picture of Birmingham* had stated that the house and grounds, 'once a favourite resort' were now deserted as unfashionable. Whatever the case, soon the inexorable advance of Birmingham threatened this rural location.

By the mid-nineteenth century both Ashted and 'Duddestown Town' with its thoroughfare of Great Lister Street were well developed and developers were looking keenly at the gardens of Vauxhall. At last in 1850 they succumbed to the urban sprawl when the leisure grounds were bought by the Victoria Building Society. A final ball was held on 16 September, and at 6 a.m. the following morning as the dance ended so the first stroke of the axe bit into one of the trees which had overshadowed so many courting couples.

Buildings soon covered the former gardens. Vauxhall Road itself, running as it did along an old lane, provided the western marker of the new estate. Erskine Street indicated its southern boundary and Pitney Street its northern. Between these two new streets were cut Newdegate Street, Scott Street, and Spooner Street. Below Erskine Street were a collection of short and narrow streets that had been laid out some years before. These were Vauxhall Grove, Northumberland Street, Saint James's Place and Railway Terrace, later Lawford Street. To the east of the whole neighbourhood ran the London and North Western Railway.

Beyond that Duddeston Meadows flourished still and at their uppermost limit by Duddeston Mill Road the name New Vauxhall came into use. Within a few years the countryside was also evicted from this spot. Soon after the Crimean War, Inkerman Street – recalling a battle in that conflict – and Dollman Street appeared. Both ran parallel with the River Rea to the east and the railway to the west, as did the short Galton Street. Going across them were Cathcart Street and Alma Crescent, also recalling a battle in the Crimea.

Galton Street recalled the intriguing and remarkable Birmingham Quaker family, which contrary to the pacifist beliefs of the Society of Friends, made its money from gunmaking. In 1777, Samuel Galton took out a lease for 99 years for the corn mill and attached buildings owned by Sir Lister Holte in Duddeston. There he built a mansion house which in 1866 became Saint Anne's School, Devon Street.

Back to backs in Saint James's Place, Vauxhall about 1906.

Mr J. H. McLaughlan was born at 45, Great Brook Street on 5 August 1918, not far from Saint James's Church, the church hall of which was on the corner of Vauxhall Road and Great Brook Street. He spent his youth locally 'till I was about 12 years old. Then my family moved to Alum Rock. I can remember the area very well. I went to school at St Vincent's RC School Great Brook Street. Very old buildings.

'In the 1926 General Strike the marchers on their way to London came along Great Brook Street. The Army Barracks was just past Saint James's Church and when near the main gates of the barracks the police and army charged out to halt the marchers. The trams ran along Ashted Row with police by the drivers during the strike.'

Phoebe Clifton, once of Erskine Street, makes a plea for the survival of the name Vauxhall 'which seems to have gone now and it's called Nechells. This used to seem a long way to me when I lived in Vauxhall.'

Samuel's granddaughter Mrs Schimmelpennick recalled that this house, confusingly called Duddeston Hall and Dudson House, had a pond 'or rather the lake, since the stream on which Birmingham stands runs through it. This lake occupied four or five acres and was of considerable length. It was truly beautiful, its borders indented, and clothed with the finest willows and poplars I have ever saw. The stillness was delightful, interrupted only by some sparkling leaping fish, or the swallow skimming in circles over the water, the hissing of the swans from their two woody islets, or the cries of the wild fowl from the far off sedges and bullrushes.'

Samuel's son, another Samuel, was a leading member of the Lunar Society and married into the Barclay banking family. Later he moved to Great Barr Hall. This was leased from the Scotts and could explain Scott Street in Vauxhall. Despite these links, the urbanised Vauxhall was a thriving working-class neighbourhood whose people played their part in the making of Birmingham as much as did the grand and wealthy.

Mary Gaden, nee Mason, came out of Northumberland Street opposite the Co-op Dairy shown in this photo of Vauxhall Road. The dairy is still there. Notice the milk floats parked on the left and the cobblestone road. Would this be Chichelly Street on the left, on the corner of which the building looks like a pub? Mary's brother, Ronnie, was a milkman for

the Co-op and his cart was pulled by a horse called *Trinder*. When he retired he was awarded the MBE after he had been put forward by the people of the village where he later worked. Schooling for Mary was at Bloomsbury Street and her days there were the best.

Josie Goodwin lived not too far away at 8 back of 144, Inkerman Street, Vauxhall until she was eleven. She well recalls Windsor Street School, where Mr Giles was the headmaster. Other teachers included Miss Hoppitt, Mr Spriggs and Mr Baker, whilst amongst her schoolmates were Janet Muslin and her sister, Patty Bowles, Marion Burtwhistle, Geoffrey Baker, Pauline Brown 'from the flats in Barrack Street and a boy called Underhill whose dad had a fruit and veg stall in the Bull Ring. They also lived in Lawley Street by the Bowles family.'

Vauxhall Road was a hive of activity as recalled by Josie. Coming along from Lawley Street there was a coffee house 'and a little shop, a park with a park keeper, the Co-op dairy, St Vincent's RC School and more flats.

'Then we go down the road and there was a pub at the top of Erskine Street. Go under the Railway bridge and Dolman Street is on the left. Toon's on one corner and a café on the other. Then Saint John's Church run by Mr Godfrey. I went three times on a Sunday and was in the choir.'

In Inkerman Street itself amongst the pubs, factories and houses was Grannie Disternal's shop by the bomb peck. 'She had a daughter called Ethel and sold sweets, bread etc but also at the back of the shop she had a big drum filled with paraffin and we used to take our can and fetch paraffin off her'.

Josie also has vivid memories of how her dad treated her asthma, for he used to take her to Saltley Gas Works and 'up the iron staircase and at the top of the gas works was a pot filled with sulphur and he used to make me breathe it in. It was vile, but it did the trick and I could breathe afterwards'.

Mysteries of Yardley Past

When I was young I always wondered why Yardley Wood was so far away from Yardley and why Yardley Grammar was on the Warwick Road in Tyseley and Yardley Secondary School was nearby in Reddings Lane. Then when I went on to big school, as we called it then, I was fascinated by a map placed on the wall of our main corridor at Moseley Grammar and which indicated that our school fell within the boundaries of the Yardley Charity. That led to another question, why should a school in Moseley be connected with Yardley?

Years later, I began reading books on old Birmingham, and especially those by two of the most important researchers into our history: Victor Skipp and John Morris Jones. Their works explained the puzzles in my mind. Until 1911, Yardley had been a separate local authority and it was much greater then the present districts of Yardley and South Yardley. Long and narrow, the ancient and strangely-shaped parish of Yardley stretched along the River Cole all the way from the Sticky Ford, Stechford, to Yardley Wood – but at no point was it more than two and a half miles wide.

Despite its narrowness, it was still a large area, covering eleven and a half square miles and within its boundaries it included the modern districts of Stechford, Yardley itself, Glebe Farm, Lea Hall, Kitt's Green, South Yardley, Hay Mills, Greet, Sparkhill, Tyseley, Acock's Green, Fox Hollies, Hall Green, Springfield, Billesley, Yardley Wood, the Wake Green district of Moseley and part of the Warstock. This elongated parish was surrounded by the parishes of Aston, King's Norton, Solihull, Lyndon (part of Bickenhill) and Sheldon and its origins are shrouded in the mysteries of the Dark Ages.

In the early 400s the Roman troops were pulled out of the province of Britannia, what is now England and Wales, and this was followed by an invasion of Angles, Saxons and Jutes. Quickly, these Germanic tribes from the borders of modern Germany and Denmark took over much of the land on the south coast, setting up little kingdoms. Despite a fight back from the British that stemmed the Anglo-Saxon tide for a generation or more, the newcomers moved inexorably westwards. By the early 500s Angles from East Anglia had invaded the Midlands. Moving up rivers like the Trent, groups of Angles began to strike out in search of land. One was headed by a man called Beorma, who with his 'ingas', people, set up a 'ham', estate, that now is called Birmingham.

Within a few decades, Beorma's people and other tribes and folk groups had been pulled into a new kingdom called Mercia. To the south was another kingdom called Hwicce, which it is believed to have been Saxon. Yardley was on the boundaries of the two. In the past it was thought that the area had been settled by Anglians because in the early Middle Ages, Yardley's church was a chapelry of Aston Parish Church which was firmly in Mercia. However, other historians believe that Yardley was established by Saxons who belonged to the Hwicce. This belief is given weight by the fact that Yardley fell under the bishopric of Worcester, which had been set up specifically to cover the Hwicce, and not to the diocese of Lichfield which was Mercian and Anglian.

However, perhaps the reality is not so stark. As a borderland area, it is probable that Yardley was settled by Anglians and Saxons and it is likely that both groups intermarried with the local British, the Welsh as we would call them today. Whatever its origins, the earliest mention of Yardley is in a document from 972, when it was given as Gyrdleah and which showed that it belonged to the Abbey of Pershore. In Old English Gyrdleah meant the wood or clearing ('leah') where rods or spars ('gyrd') are got. Another possibility put forward by Victor Skipp is that 'gyrd' meant a yard, and in the Anglo-Saxon period this could also indicate a quarter of an acre and thus a small plot of land. In this case, Gyrdleah would be the small clearing.

Yardley comes to notice again in the Domesday Book of 1086 when it was given as Gerlei but because it was a member of Beoley, which belonged to Pershore Abbey, it was not recorded separately. Consequently, it is not possible to work out exact figures as regards land in use, plough teams and population. However, John Morris Jones felt that the manor had a population of about 60 and that about 600 acres of it was under cultivation. That was a third of its total area.

In the succeeding years, folk from Yardley struck out to make more clearings at Billesley, Hay Mills and Lea Hall, and by the late Middle Ages an open field system was obvious in Yardley and Lee. Early in the thirteenth century, Yardley's connection with Beoley lapsed and within a hundred years, so too had the overlordship of Pershore Abbey.

By the late fifteenth century Yardley was owned by the king and in 1629, Sir Richard Grevis of Moseley bought the title of the lord of the manor - now recalled in Grevis Road, Yardley. He owned wide lands elsewhere, in Castle Bromwich, Little Bromwich, Bordesley, Sutton Coldfield, Sheldon and Bickenhill (then spelt Bicknell in the manner that it was pronounced until recently). The connection with Moseley continued, for in 1766, the manor of Yardley was purchased by John Taylor, who had already bought Moseley Hall and much of its estate. The famous Brummagem button king, he was the co-founder of Taylor and Lloyd's bank. Taylor's descendants disposed of most of their holdings in Yardley at about the time of the First World War.

At the turn of the nineteenth century, the whole parish of Yardley had a population of just 2,000 and it did not increase substantially until after the 1850s. From 1871 to 1911, the number of people doubled itself every decade, but most of this spectacular growth occurred in Sparkhill, Greet, Tyseley and Hay Mills. Indeed after Yardley became a Rural District Council in 1892, steps were eventually taken to open a council house in Sparkhill. The modern districts of Yardley and South Yardley remained sparsely populated and rural in appearance - although a number of grand houses lined Church Road and Stoney Lane.

Now an integral part of Birmingham, Yardley and its many districts did not become part of Birmingham until 1911. By the First World War, changes were becoming obvious. The 'Swan' Yardley had become the focus of a large number of terraced houses built for the better-paid of the working class and Preston Road, Gladstone Road and others had appeared. A small development at the 'Yew Tree' had been laid out in a similar fashion, as had Sir John Holder's Redhill Estate between Deakin's Road and Holder Road. Urbanisation speeded up after 1919 and during the inter-war years the land close to Saint Edburgha's, Yardley Parish Church, was laid out by private builders mostly with semi-detached houses. This led to the filling in of open spaces beyond Church Road and the emergence of Farnol Road and others.

To the north of Stoney Lane the corporation took over Fast Pits Farm, at the bottom of Wash Lane and close to Holder Road, and Wash Mill Farm, on Hob Moor Lane by The Ring. This land reached to Bordesley Green in the east and it was called the Marlborough House and Fast Pits Farm Estate. On it the corporation built the large total of 2,171 houses; whilst in that part of South Yardley across the Coventry Road, the land of Moat Farm and Highfield Farm was mostly taken over by private builders who formed roads between Clay Lane and Gilberstone Road.

Since the inter-war years much of old Yardley has disappeared beneath the march of new housing, but just off the busy Number 11 route and in the aptly named Church Road lies the old Yardley Village. It is a small, pedestrianised conservation area with the Trust School and a fine parish church of red sandstone taken, undoubtedly, from the earth of Yardley. This church is dedicated to Saint Edburgha, a granddaughter of King Alfred. The legend goes that from when she was little, Edburgha was very religious and one day her father, King Edward the Elder, offered her glittering jewels and gold in one had and a Gospel book and chalice in the other. She readily took the latter and became a nun. After her death she was buried in

Rural Yardley in 1937. A view from the tower of Yardley Parish Church showing fields which soon would be covered with council housing.

Children racing in Yardley Park as part of the celebrations locally for the Diamond Jubilee of Queen Victoria in 1897.

Winchester, the capital of the Anglo-Saxon kingdom of Wessex, but later some of her remains were taken to Pershore Abbey, to which Yardley belonged, and it is said some then came to Saint Edburgha's Church.

There is evidence of a chapel in Yardley from the late 1100s, but the oldest part of the church as seen today is the chancel, dating back to about 1200. The nave and transepts are early fourteenth century; the north aisle came a few decades later; whilst the porch, tower and vestry are from the fifteenth century. With its tall and proud spire, Saint Edburgha's is the proud possessor of one of the best peals of eight bells in the United Kingdom – giving its name to the nearby 'Ring o' Bells' pub. Inside the church there is a Jacobean pulpit and an incised slab from the tomb of Thomas Este.

The Este or Est family appeared in Yardley from the early fifteenth century. As Victor Skipp's meticulous research reveals they were amongst a number of families that had a deep effect upon the parish from the last years of the Middle Ages. Amongst the others were the Dolphins, hence Dolphin Road, Acock's Green; the Flavells, recalled in Flavell Road, Yardley; and the Greswoldes, brought to mind in Greswolde Road, Springfield.

This Este presence was founded by Thomas, the valet of King Henry VI. He married Marion, the daughter of William Del Hay and so acquired Hay Hall, which is still in Redfern Road, Tyseley. He and his wife are shown in the top of the incised alabaster tomb chest. He has short hair and pointed shoes, whilst his wife is at prayer and wears a heart-shaped head-dress. The Este family was present in Yardley until the eighteenth century and are brought to mind by Este Road.

The Foliots were also connected with the church and have Foliot Fields named after them. Aylmer Foliot of Pershore came into possession of Blakesley Hall through his marriage to the granddaughter of Richard Smallbroke, the man who had the hall built. Aylmer himself gave a cottage and certain lands to Yardley Church and also property called Deepmoors.

There are other fascinating road names in Yardley and South Yardley. Until 1907 Amington Road was called Tanyard Lane, after the Yardley Tannery started by George Muscott in 1884. His company continued making high quality shoe leather until the mid-1960s. As with all tanyards, the smell was strong and unappealing. Consequently, Tanyard Lane may have given negative impressions so that the name was changed to Amington Road. Not far away is Graham Road. This was known as Madcap Lane or Madcat Lane, until 1927. Its new name refers to George Graham who moved to the Oaklands on the Coventry Road in the 1870s and whose family was involved in the Yardley Stud Farm, hence Stud Lane. And what of Workhouse Lane, which shifted into Holder Road in 1898 and Moses Lane, which was transformed into Croft Road the year before?

The past may appear to be hidden in Yardley, but let your eyes roam thoughtfully and it can be seen. It's there in the church of Saint Edburgha, in a variety of road names, in the medieval ridge and furrow in the park behind the church, in the pathway across Kent's Moat Park which follows the ancient Dagardingweg, an Anglo Saxon road, and in its name of Yardley itself.

The old and the new. A delivery man with his horse and cart at the island in Barrows Lane, Yardley in 1951. Thanks to the Birmingham Evening Mail.

Chapter 3
Hard Collar

Stick to Your Business and Advertise: Bird's Custard

Alfred Bird had a keen and analytical mind – and on top of that he was ambitious. He'd served his time with the well-respected Birmingham druggist firm of Philip Harris and Co and had qualified as a Fellow of the Chemists Society and now he was ready to set up on his own. In 1837 and at the relatively young age of 24, the newly-married chemist opened up shop in Bell Street, in the heart of the Bull Ring. With his small signboard hanging up outside proclaiming his name and business, he carried on his trade selling toiletries - but that was not enough for Alfred's inquiring nature. His real passion was for experimental chemistry, for investigating new processes and improving old ones.

Things seemed to progress well enough, but it was Alfred's determination to help his wife, Elizabeth, which led him to found a major business. Not much is known about this woman, bar for the fact that she had digestive problems. In particular, yeast-based products upset her. This difficulty set her husband thinking and experimenting to find a way to allow his wife to eat bread without discomfort. In 1843, Alfred cracked it. He came up with a yeast substitute that he called Bird's Fermenting Powder. Later known as Bird's Baking Powder, the product was seen by many as making a bread that was light and highly satisfactory.

Next, Alfred turned his attention to something else that bedevilled his wife. Like many folk, Elizabeth was fond of custard, which was made from a mixture of eggs and milk. The snag was that Elizabeth was allergic to eggs. Alfred's aim was now to perfect an eggless custard. He did so and began an association so strong that for generations when people heard the name Bird's then custard powder sprang to mind and when they thought of custard then Bird's came into their head. This custard powder that did away with eggs was based on cornflour – and as good as the real thing to eat, yet it was quicker and easier to prepare.

Word spread fast around Brum about Alfred's wonderful new products and determined to get them to a wider market, the inventor brought out a calendar on which was praised the benefits of Bird's Baking Powder and which was given away free. It seems that this was the first instance anywhere of such an advertising ploy. Within ten years of opening his first shop, Alfred's business had so prospered that he moved to bigger premises nearby in Worcester Street. Here he hung a simple but effective motto: 'Early to Bed, Early to Rise, Stick to Your Work and Advertise'.

The centenary advert for Bird's Custard Powder.

Increasingly his baking and custard powder were sold nationally and then in 1855, this entrepreneurial chemist decided to take a big jump. He wrote to the War Department, offering to provide baking powder to the British soldiers fighting in the Crimean War. This would give them the chance of proper bread instead of almost unpalatable hard tack biscuits, and would also enable the baking of cakes and puddings for the wounded and ill.

It was the Duke of Newcastle who was in charge of matters. He stated that he wanted to see a loaf made from the baking powder and to ensure that there was no trickery, he declared that the loaf should be prepared and baked in front of competent authorities. So with the Mayor of Birmingham watching him, Alfred did as he was bid. He made five loaves, upon the covering of one of which was stamped the seal of Birmingham Corporation. The duke was impressed and praised the loaf as sweet and good. After surmounting more formalities, Alfred began supplying his baking powder and later in life he often stated that he liked to think that his baking powder had been used to bake bread and cakes for Florence Nightingale to take around those she cared for.

Enthusiastic about other experiments, Alfred made a huge water barometer in his shop. This allowed him to deliver a paper on atmospheric pressure behaviour during storms to the Philosophical Society. He also developed a night light that could be filled safely with oil whilst it was still alight. But Alfred's future and that of his son was to lie not with such investigations but with the powders he had devised. Indeed, it was Alfred Frederick Bird who drove the family business forward.

He joined the company when he was eighteen and he soon made an impact. In the early 1870s he devised Bird's Blancmange Powder. Adventurously, he launched it with fourteen flavours that included exotic tastes such as nectarine. In the decade following his father's death in 1879, Alfred enthusiastically grasped the new medium of pictorial advertising. This was crucial in making Bird's grow and become a household name. The Worcester Street building was expanded but still it was too small for the rising business. Consequently, Alfred took on a new factory in Moor Street. He moved into it all his machinery, materials, stocks and books. But just before the place opened, a major fire destroyed everything.

Undaunted by this major set-back, Alfred dug into his reserves of cash and in 1887 built the first section of the Devonshire Works in Floodgate Street. In the succeeding years, it became bigger as business continued to increase. This was due to Alfred's thirst for new products such as Bird's Egg Substitute for cake making and, in 1895, Bird's Jelly Crystals. Small competitors picked up Alfred's ideas but he refused to be drawn into the trap of lowering standards to match their low prices. Quality was as much his trademark as were innovation and perseverance.

As the twentieth century dawned, the new company of Alfred Bird and Sons Ltd was formed. Two of Alfred Frederick's sons, Robert and Geoffrey, were active in the business and his two others were on the board of directors. Shortly after, in 1905, the making of toiletries and chemists sundries was discontinued so that Bird's could focus on the food side of affairs. A pioneer of convenience foods, Bird's added to their list of products mixtures for buns and cakes, steamed puddings, tea cake and Yorkshire Puddings.

Bird's workers off on a charabanc trip to Stratford. Thanks to J. Lambley.

Pauline Franklin was a proud Brummie who often wrote to me about her experiences and her love of our city. Sadly, she has passed on but she will always be remembered because she made sure that her memories and photos will be brought forward to generations yet to come. Pauline began with the company in 1957 in the invoicing departments 'and during this time Bird's had delivered the first computer in Birmingham. It was so big that it had to be installed on a Sunday whilst the police closed one side of the road in Digbeth.

'The huge monster was hauled up the front of the building to the second floor where the windows had to be taken out. It was treated with the greatest of care and had to have a special room temperature. Most people were against having it because around 100 people were made redundant. I recall that we were all asked if we would like to take the computer exam and I decided to have a go. We had to attend the Chamber of Commerce in Harborne Road were we were tested all day. The idea was to see if you could survive under pressure and I nearly did not.

'During the afternoon session my mind went a complete blank and I could not think of anything. I looked out of the winder until my brain started to function again. I passed with enough points to apply for a job connected with the computer, but decided it was not my cup of tea. It was not long before we realised that, marvellous as the computer was, it had not got the power to think or notice something was wrong, especially when hundreds of invoices were sent out far in excess of what they should have been.'

The mother of Carol Evans worked for Bird's before and during the Second World War. Ethel Jackson, nee Whitehouse, remembered that one of her favourite jobs was pulling the jelly from the moulds because this made her hands lovely and soft on account of the glycerine contained in the jelly. Before the Christmas of 1937, two raffles were held in the factory: one for the office staff and the other for the shop floor workers. The winner from each section had the privilege to sit either side of Mr Bird at the annual Christmas dinner. Ethel won the shop floor ticket. During the course of the meal she asked if her employer would sign her menu card, which he did.

In the war, and after a full day's work, Ethel sang operetta as a member of a wartime concert party. She and colleagues would be taken by coach to various venues around the Midlands. Sometimes they were blindfolded. In addition to performing their own act, each member 'would all muck in and help with the costumes, make-up and scenery. Afterwards they were usually invited to the officers' mess where they indulged in the most marvellous food: beef, hams, fresh fruit, jams etc. None of these items, of course, were ever seen in the shops during the war. It was usual for some of this food to be smuggled out as a treat for family members.'

With his success, Alfred Frederick turned to politics and was elected to parliament as the Conservative member for Wolverhampton West. Robert took control of matters and brought in salesmen and window display experts. Then in 1922, came an eye-catching move. Silver packaging was dropped and the new packets were made distinctive by broad bands of red, yellow and blue.

Bird's managed to come through the hard years of the 1920s and the depression of the early 1930s, and the Devonshire Works survived the Blitz on Birmingham that devastated the area around. Then in 1944, the General Foods Corporation of America approached Bird's to cooperate in making Grape Nuts, a ready-to-eat breakfast cereal, and Maxwell House Ground Coffee. Three years later, Birds was taken over by its American partner, although the company carried on under its own name with Sir Robert as chairman.

At the same time the old Fisher and Ludlow factory in Bradford Street was acquired for the production of Grape Nuts and other goods. It was called the Miller Works after the American who negotiated the deal to acquire Bird's. One of the most successful new items emerged in 1954. This was Bird's Instant Whip, based on the American Jell-O Instant Pudding and which led to the development of Bird's Dream Topping and Bird's Angel Delight. In the same year English tastes for beverages were transformed by the introduction of Maxwell House Instant Coffee. At first this was brought into Birmingham where it was packaged, but from 1956 the Miller Works was producing the coffee itself.

Ironically, the tremendous impact of this coffee and of Bird's own goods led to the end of production in Birmingham. The company was concerned that it had no room for expansion in the city and a destructive fire in 1962 at the Devonshire Works precipitated a move to Banbury. Four years later the new plant was up and running and half of Bird's workforce of 600 had moved to Oxfordshire. So ended the bond between Birmingham and Bird's.

Minting the Coins. The Birmingham Mint

Ralph Heaton must have been a headstrong, determined and forceful young man. Apprenticed to a brassfounder in Birmingham, he had a dispute with his gaffer and like so many lads went off and took the king's shilling. That's how Ralph came to be in Gibraltar with the army in 1782. Britain was really up against it. Both the French and Spanish had sided with Washington's Americans who were battling for independence. Faced with a powerful coalition and fighting across several continents, the British were taking a pasting.

One of the main aims of the Spanish and French was to capture Gibraltar. Surrounded by enemy territory and the sea, the British troops were outnumbered eight to one, but successfully resisted a four year siege - and, according to family history, Ralph Heaton played a vital role in keeping the Union Flag flying over The Rock. The garrison was tormented by floating bombardment vessels. They had wooden walls that were seven foot thick that could withstand British salvoes. But Heaton came up

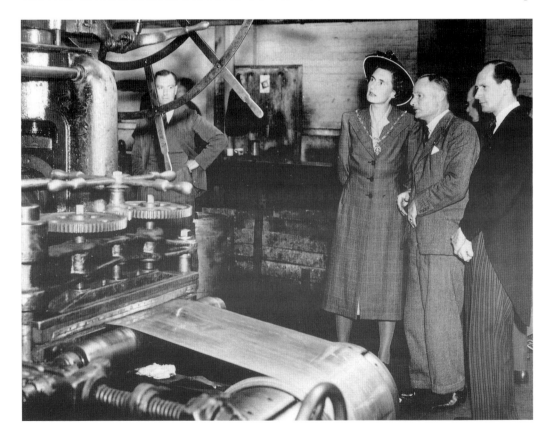

The Lord Mayor of Birmingham, Councillor John Charles Burman, and the Lady Mayoress with Mr Brezena, the managing director of the Birmingham Mint, watching the machine rolling of copper in 1948. Thanks to the Birmingham Evening Mail.

with an idea to end the attacks. Instead of trying to batter the vessels, he suggested that the British gunners ought to fire red hot shot, which would set the floating batteries alight. During a day and night of continuous bombardment, ten of the enemy vessels were destroyed and Heaton was praised by General Elliott, who led the dogged defence of Gibraltar.

After he left the Army, Ralph Heaton came back to Brum and set up as a brassfounder in 1794. His imaginative mind and hard work led him to do well and one of the things he came up with was a machine for cutting out biscuits for the Royal Navy. Ralph was joined in business by his sons - John, William, George, Ralph and Reuben - and together the family moved into making stamped brass ornaments and fittings for furniture, beds and curtain mountings and also the manufacture of brooches and ornamental buttons.

The lads were as creative as their father, and in 1833 four of them devised a steam carriage that ran from Birmingham to Bromsgrove. The other son, Ralph, was more concerned with making die stamps and it was through this interest that he took the firm into the minting of coins - for when the die was pressed on to a blank of metal the impression that resulted formed the coin.

Birmingham's spectacular rise to acclaim as the City of 1,000 Trades owed everything to the ingenuity, inventiveness and innovation of a host of Brummie workers. With hands that cunningly fashioned metal into the finest and most useful of wares, they constantly sought out new trades as a test for their crafts. One of them was the minting of coins. This was amongst 'the curious arts' about which William Hutton, Birmingham's first historian, wrote and which were 'cultivated by the hand of genius'.

Matthew Boulton, one of the greatest figures in the history of our city, was crucial in the emergence of the art of making coins. In 1786, he set up a mint at his Soho Works for the forming of copper coins. There was a severe want of coppers as most coins were silver and soon Boulton was supplying them to British and other governments as well as to the East India Company. Boulton's successors closed this business in 1850 and his machinery was bought by Ralph Heaton II.

One of the first contracts gained by the company was from the Royal Mint in New South Wales. Between 1850 and 1866 the coins minted at the Birmingham Mint were huge in number and variety. About 2,000 tons of copper and bronze were supplied for Britain; 1,400 tons for India; 700 tons for Tunis; and 1,000 more tons together for Turkey, Hong Kong, Haiti, Sarawak, Tuscany, Venezuela, Canada and Chile. In addition, the Birmingham Mint struck 1,600 tons of bronze coins in Milan for the new kingdom of Italy - the blanks having been made in Brum and shipped out - whilst 750 tons was struck in Marseilles on the re-coinage of the French currency after the French Empire was re-established under Napoleon III. And in striking 1,720 tons of bronze coins for Britain alone, more than 17,000 dies were used.

From 1860, the Mint was based at its famous factory in Icknield Street and it was the site of a progressive and creative operation. Just over 100 years later, in 1967, a new mint was built and equipped in Warstone Lane, next to the main works. This formed a self contained and highly secure production unity and it increased capacity to the minting of 15 million coins a week. By this date the last of the Heatons associated with the business had retired, although descendants of the family remain in the West Midlands. Then, in 1992, workers at the Mint perfected the production of nickel-plated coins, exemplifying the way in which a traditional Birmingham industry was adept at reacting and adapting to changing circumstances and the new demands of customers.

A craft is like a memory. Once it is allowed to disappear it is gone forever. Unfortunately that craft was allowed to disappear from Birmingham in 2003. The Mint's workers were as skilled as ever, their machinery was sought after and the business could have continued. But through a combination of external factors the Birmingham Mint was laid low and is no more. This article, then, is written in tribute to the workers of the Birmingham Mint, a pioneering and successful company that should not have been allowed to close.

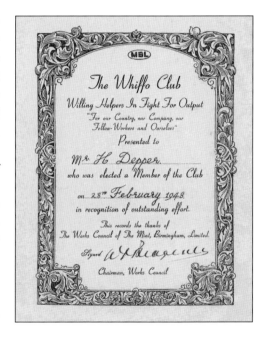

The Whiffo certificate of June Depper's Dad. June's family was Birmingham Mint through and through. Her dad had a job there about 1937. She recalls: 'He had always been in the building trade working outdoors and when the weather was bad they didn't get paid if they were laid off. In 1936 I arrived, Mom and Dad's first born, and they were very hard up - as a lot of people were - but Dad decided that he would look for work indoors. I don't know how many jobs he applied for but he finished up at The Mint. What a good move that was. Dad was on maintenance work, which meant anything to so with brick work he did and lots more besides. He was also an ARP warden at the factory during the war.

'There was always a summer outing for the workers' children and we always had a wonderful time. Mr Brezena, who I think was probably the Factory Manager, was there each time to wave us off. We also had great Christmas parties. There was one man who belonged to the Magic Circle and he would amaze us. One of his tricks was to produce coins from behind his ears.'

Eric Barker was 'very sorry to hear about the closure of the Mint. I was employed at the Mint for about 20 years as maintenance electrician. My brother, Wilfred Barker, worked there from a lad and became over the wages office. I had many working days at the Mint, it's called the mint family. June Depper's Dad, Harry, was a mate of mine, I knew the family, went to his home many times. Harry Depper and Harry Higgs and two more chaps used to brick all furnaces. Harry Depper knew the drainage like the back of his hand; he left once and they asked him to come back.

'*The Mint had a boxing club, football team, cricket team, they had their own sports field, also British Legion branch. We had a team which ran the Bingo twice a week, Ivor Griffiths from the tube mill office ran it, from the proceeds we sent the pensioners on one week's holiday, the work's nurse, nurse Wade, and other helpers went also. The Mint had a work's council, which met once a month on a Saturday morning, with reps from each department and management. One thing they did was to nominate workers for an award called 'Whiffo' - willing helper in fight for output. Those who got the award received a certificate, a badge and money; it went up one star, two star and the money went up too.*

'*Mr Brezena was managing director, Mr King was works manager. Mr Brezena came in of a morning walked right through the works and called most of them by their names - Jack, Tom! I had one of the Mint's houses opposite the works, back to back house. I had the bad luck to lose my wife in 1958, having our third child, Mr Brezena told me any time I wanted to go over to the kids to go, that is the sort of person he was.*

'*We had a good maintenance crew, fitters, bricklayers, painters, and electricians. I often think about some of them and wonder where they are now, especially the electricians like Bill Harris, Tony Quirk, John Stone, Peter Stanton, Eric Wyate, Lofty and others.*'

Working at the Mint in the 1950s. Thanks to the Birmingham Evening Mail. The father, of Mrs Jeynes, Thomas Hunter, 'worked at the Mint for most of his life, after his part in the First World War, he never lost a day's work. I used to go to the Christmas parties in the canteen up the iron staircase. Every Saturday evening my Dad would take me to watch the boxing matches, he would take me into a room at the back of the boxing ring to see what the prizes would be for the winners. I remember seeing a lovely brass fender there and my Dad said the boxer "Bunny Mason" would definitely be taking that home to his mother that night and sure enough he did. They were happy times, I had a tour of the B'ham Mint factory courtesy of my Dad and was fascinated to watch all the foreign coins come flying down a chute at the side of the machine.'

Workers at the Mint in the 1950s. Thanks to the Birmingham Evening Mail. Doreen Palmer's Grandfather, Fred Lane, 'worked at the Mint for many years, I cannot give you the number of years but I do know that he retired age 65 in 1954 and was given a grandmother clock for his services to the Mint. I do not know what his actual job was but I do know that he trained a team of boxers for the Mint (Johnny Mann being one of his claims to fame). I remember my Grandmother and myself used to accompany him to the boxing matches in the Mint canteen, he also used to box himself and I am still in possession of one of his prizes, a cut glass vase. He also ran the football team at the Mint, their home matches were played at a sports ground which, I believe, belonged to the Mint in Warstock.

'Grandfather used to mow and roll the pitches at the ground, which had a pavilion on the grounds. We, as a family, spent many happy hours at this ground, it was like being out in the country, there was a farmer nearby who, when we were visiting, used to bring vegetables and eggs to my Grandmother, his name was Mr Cutts. Also by the ground was a quarry which had a house right on the edge, we all expected it to have disappeared each time we went there, we believed it to be haunted. My Grandmother used to wash the football kit alternate weeks sharing with another. My Grandfather

also assisted with the running of the annual sports day which took place at the ground in Warstock and all the Mint workers and their children came along to join in the fun and games. Grandfather also played cricket for the Mint as did my Father.

'My mother also worked for the Mint for many years, retiring with ill health, her name was May Siviter but she was always known as May Lane, she worked on a foot press and was on the work's council for many years and I believe that June Depper's father Harry worked alongside with Mom. She helped to organize the outings and Christmas parties for both the young and old, pensioners used to go to Blackpool for a week. Mr William Brezena was the Managing Director at this time and as June said he was always there to see the children off on their trips, he, in actual fact, gave me one of two references needed when I left school to work at Boots The Chemist in 1952.

'Mom also used to organize concerts and pantomimes, which took place in the Mint canteen, along with my father Fred Siviter (Jim) who also worked for the Mint. The troupe of which I was a member was called The Rhythm Rascals and was run by Mrs Sayce and Nora, who was her sister, it was lovely to appear on stage and to receive love letters from the boys in the audience (I was only about seven). I still have two photographs of the troupe when we performed Cinderella. When I was about 20 with one of the troupe member Joyce Roberts we started a tap dancing class in the Mint canteen every Friday night, the person in charge of the canteen at this time was Cora.

'Other members of my family to work at the Mint was my Grandfather's brother Albert Lane he worked in the time office, my Mother's brother Fred Lane he worked in B department and my brother Clive Siviter who worked in the laboratory.'

Digbeth Wells to Elan Valley. Brum's Water

'Water, water everywhere nor any drop to drink'. These are famous lines from Samuel Taylor Coleridge's 'Rime of the Ancient Mariner', telling of a ship and its company becalmed upon the ocean and with its supply of fresh water running out. Surrounded by water as they were and tempted as much as they were, not one drop of that water could be drunk because of its salt content. For all its literary worth and its lack of connection to our city, that line has a powerful resonance for the people of Birmingham's back-to-back neighbourhoods in the nineteenth century. With rivers like the Rea, streams like the Hockley Brook, and a host of wells sunk into Birmingham's high water table, there was plenty of drinking water in the town but little of it that was fit to drink.

In 1845 Robert Slaney enquired into *The State of Birmingham and Other Towns*. He described how each yard had often had wash-house (brew'us) and sometimes an ash-pit (miskins) 'and always one or two privies, or sets of privies, close to which there is often one or more pigsties full of hog-wash and heaps of offensive manure'. In the middle of each yard 'there stands a pump for the inhabitants. These courts are frequently unpaved, and the open channel for dirty water ill-defined, so that stagnant puddles in wet weather are the consequence.' These problems were made worse because 'the overflowings from the privy-vaults, pigsties and dirt-heaps' trickled down the yards, passing close to the well 'and no doubt often enter it'. As if that was not bad enough, the yards were mostly unpaved, uncleansed and unswept.

Six years later, Charles Mackay, a correspondent for the *Morning Chronicle* in London also wrote about the sanitary conditions in Birmingham. In the course of his investigations he went to Myrtle Row, in Greens Village – later cleared for the cutting of John Bright Street – and a neighbourhood of Irish folk from County Roscommon. There was one water pump for 53 three-roomed back-to-back houses. Mackay noted that the pump that drew water from a well was 'at the extremity of the row. There had been a second pump at the other end, but it rotted away, and the property of these fifty-three dwellings being divided between three owners who could not agree amongst themselves, the pump had not been repaired.'

Between 300 and 400 people lived in Myrtle Row and the water they pumped up was 'of a greenish colour, and smelling strongly of gas as if a gas-pipe had burst, and were emitting a stream through it'. A woman told the reporter that the water was filthy stuff and there was not enough of it to wash the house. For drinking she had buy water at a ha'penny a can. These dismal circumstances were common across working-class Birmingham, so that stale and brackish water was taken from butts that collected rain water or bought from water carts that were driven around the streets and which drew their supplies from wells in and around Digbeth.

Matters improved little in the succeeding years, as was revealed by a Sanitary Census of Birmingham carried out in late 1874 and early 1875. The best-quality houses locally were excluded, leaving 70,561 that were taken into account. Of these

24,000 'were dependent for their water supply on wells liable to be corrupted by the percolation of surface matter from middens and ashpits, while 101 had no water supply at all'. This Census was taken during the mayoralty of radical Joe, Joseph Chamberlain, and it was he who was to provide the impetus for serious, long-lasting and effective reform.

Folk in a yard in Thomas Street, about 1882, showing the dreadful conditions endured by the poor of Birmingham. As elsewhere in working-class Birmingham, the residents drew water from dirty wells. Soon after this photo was taken, this street was cleared to make way for Corporation Street.

Brian Henderson was drawn by this photo. He had 'only ever seen a British half-farthing in a library book. Then I saw one recently and bought it. As I rode home on the train I read your Evening Mail article "Water, Water, everywhere . . ." which made me think about the value of this coin from 1844 and of the people who had to use them. It was seven years after that date that a woman told reporter Charles Mackay she "had to buy (drinking) water in Birmingham at a ha'penny a can". In those days of the "gold standard" coinage, the half-farthing was of very low value indeed. Being one-eighth of a penny and with 240 pennies to the pound (or sovereign), the half farthing was 1/1920th of a pound and 1/2016th part of a guinea (or 21/-).

'It is not the mathematics which touches me, but the fact that these "mites" had an even smaller value than some Indian coins (pice) which British soldiers of the 1940s used as washers, and that some people in Victorian days had to rely on them.'

Fresh water – often regarded as a basic human right and as often out of the reach of the poor. So it was in Birmingham until Radical Joe took control of Birmingham between 1873 and 76. Dynamic, decisive and determined, Chamberlain so transformed Birmingham that it threw off its negative image as 'blackest Brummagem' and grabbed for itself the title of 'the best-governed city in the world'. Infused with the belief that the municipality owed a duty to improve life for all its citizens, Chamberlain embarked upon a policy of municipal socialism. A capitalist and an entrepreneur yet he was convinced that the Corporation ought to control the services that were essential for the good health of the people of Birmingham.

To this end, Chamberlain and his supporters who had taken over the Council implemented a variety of far-reaching and positive measures. A bye-law was passed that effectively forbade the building of back-to-back houses; the sewerage farm at Saltley was extended and improved; a drainage board was established; unhealthy midden privies were replaced by dry pan closets (lavatories with a pan underneath); wooden tubs for the collection of rubbish were put in each yard; a Medical Officer of Health was appointed who reported to a Health Committee; and sanitary inspectors were taken on to deal with a variety of nuisances – from adulterated food to filthy courts.

Under the revolutionary new regime, the private gas and water companies were municipalised and landlords were forced to close polluted wells and connect their properties via a standpipe to the town water supply. Dr Hill, the Medical Officer of Health, was enjoined to inspect the wells of Birmingham. The results were damning. In almost all instances, the hundreds of wells inspected were polluted with sewage, through surface drainage, which rendered the water unfit for drinking. As a result, in the nine years from 1876 almost 3,000 wells supplying about 60,000 people were closed.

As for the town water, it was taken from the supplies of the private Birmingham Waterworks Company. This was authorised by Act of Parliament in 1826 to cover Birmingham and the Parish of Aston. The company developed slowly, taking five years to make a reservoir at Aston for water from the River Tame. By 1859, water was also taken from the Hawthorn Brook in Witton and the Perry Brook.

Over the next decade or so the company extended its operations to King's Norton, Yardley, Harborne, Northfield, Handsworth and Sutton Coldfield, which latter move necessitated the taking of water from Plant's Brook Forge. Wells were also sunk in Oscott, Perry, Witton, Erdington and Selly Oak, whilst more water was drawn in from the Rivers Blythe and Bourne. This increase of supplies arose not only because of the widening scope of the Company but also because the water from the Tame was so polluted that after 1872 it was no longer used.

Despite its growth, the Birmingham Waterworks Company was faced by major problems. Its water was collected from various sources over a wide area and it was stored in twelve reservoirs: three in Witton; two each in Aston, Edgbaston and at Plant's Brook; and one each in Perry and Whitacre. These reservoirs led to an expensive pumping system. For example, the water stored at Aston had to be pumped from 297 feet above sea level to 532 feet at the Monument Lane Reservoir in Edgbaston and then to 602 feet at the nearby reservoir on the Hagley Road.

For all its engineering achievements and its desire to increase Birmingham's supply of fresh water, by 1875 when it was municipalised, the private water company had only 17,641 customers. This situation changed drastically following the takeover of the water supply by the City. Back in 1854, the Council had recognised that a clean water supply was vital to the health of the town and had sought to purchase the private Waterworks Company. This attempt failed. Then in 1869, another push was made at municipalisation led by Alderman Avery. He highlighted the disgusting state of the town's well water and stressed that a company motivated by profit could not meet the wants of the people of Birmingham. On the behalf of the at least 150,000 folk dependent upon foul wells, Avery declared that 'Wealth can always take care of itself, but poverty cannot; and surely it is the duty of a wise local government to endeavour to surround the humbler classes of the population with its benevolent and protecting care'.

Unfortunately, the Council did not back Avery's plans, although in 1871 the Public Works Committee instructed a Mr Rawlinson to report on a scheme for obtaining water for Birmingham. He recommended that water be taken from the Rivers Elan and Claerwen in Mid Wales. The advice was unheeded. At last in 1874, the mayor Joseph Chamberlain brought forward a resolution to the Council that a Bill should be prepared to provide either for the transfer by agreement or by compulsory purchase of the private waterworks undertaking.

He stressed that the health of large towns and the liability of their populations were connected intimately with the water supply, whilst there were special reasons why the supply of water 'to all communities should be in the hands of local representative authorities, and not in the hands of private speculators, to whom pecuniary profit must necessarily be the first consideration'. There were also financial considerations, for consumers had to pay a high interest upon the capital and loans of the company compared to the lower rates of interest at which the Corporation could borrow. Crucially Chamberlain expounded a most important principle: that whilst the municipalised gas works had to make a profit 'the waterworks should never be a source of profit, as all profit should go in reduction at the price of water'.

The Council's Bill was opposed staunchly by the Waterworks Company, but Chamberlain proved persuasive. He told the Commons Committee that discussed the matter that he was certain that 'the power of life and death should not be left in the hands of a commercial company, but should be conducted by the representatives of the people'. The Bill was passed on 7 August 1875.

Over the next few years, improvements were made to the town's supply, including a new reservoir at Shustoke, but increasingly the Council became aware of the difficulties with the local supply. Back in 1871, Robert Rawlinson had stated that the area covered by the Waterworks Company had the potential to yield a sufficient supply for 50 years, although the water was excessively hard and polluted and would become more contaminated. In these circumstances, he had recommended taking water from the Rivers Elan and Claerwen in mid Wales.

Rawlinson's ambitious scheme was not adopted, but in 1890 the Council was forced to look at its supplies. Demand for water was rising rapidly, whilst the Corporation had reached the limits of its borrowings. James Mansergh was engaged to report on new sources of water. He had been one of the engineers who had assisted Rawlinson and he concluded that to obtain a thoroughly satisfactory supply of water, the Council had to go across the border to Wales, where the water from the Elan and Clearwen rivers was the best.

The Elan Valley had a number of other advantages. Its average rainfall of 1830mm compared to that of London's 593mm and Edinburgh's 676mm. Narrow downstream valleys locally made the building of dams easier. An impermeable bedrock prevented the water seeping away. And finally, because the area is mostly higher than Birmingham, through careful surveys and precise engineering the water could be moved the 73.5 miles of its journey by gravity, without the need to be pumped.

Convinced of the urgency of a new water supply, the Council introduced a Bill into Parliament in 1892. It was enacted later that year and building work began soon after in 1893. James Mansergh was encharged with the engineering works in Wales, the railways and the aqueduct from Elan to Hagley. The rest of the scheme was entrusted to Mr Gray, the engineer of the Water Department of the City. This included the Frankley Reservoir, the Northfield and Warley reservoirs and tanks, the Birmingham tank, the filter beds at Frankley, and the mains to and from the home reservoirs. After Gray's retirement in 1894, Mansergh took over the whole scheme.

At the Elan Valley, a railway line was laid to transport the workers and the thousands of tonnes of building material required each day. The first length of this railway was constructed by contractors. Other than this the Council itself employed the workmen, believing that the responsibility of safety, especially on the dams, was too great for a contractor. A village of wooden huts was purpose built to house most of the workers. New workers spent a night in the doss house to be deloused and examined for infectious diseases. Only then were they allowed across the river to the village. Single men lived in groups of eight in a terraced house shared with a man and his wife.

There was a hospital for injuries, an isolation hospital and a bath house which the men could use up to three times a week, but the women only once. The pub was for men only, whilst other facilities included a library, public hall, shop and canteen. There was even street lighting powered by hydroelectric generators.

The dams were built in two phases, firstly construction in the Elan Valley, opened by King Edward VII in July 1904, and later the Claerwen Dam. In total, the Elan scheme cost £6 million and employed 50,000 men. It was one of the greatest engineering achievements of the age. The building of the second phase of dams was delayed due to the First and Second World Wars. Work started again in 1946, and because of engineering advancements one large dam was built rather than three smaller ones. Six years later the Claerwen Dam was opened by Queen Elizabeth II in one of the first official engagements of her reign. Its completion nearly doubled the available water for Birmingham so that the massive amount of 300 million litres of water a day can be extracted from the Elan Valley.

At the northern end of the Elan Valley, the Craig Goch reservoir covers 217 acres with a 120 foot high dam holding back some 2,000 million gallons of water. Pen–Y-Garreg Dam is 417 feet wide with a spectacular curtain of water falling 123 feet and holds 1,320 million gallons. Garreg Ddu, bridged and flowing into Caban Coch added 8,000 million gallons. The Claerwen dam brought the total capacity to over 21,000 million gallons.

Elan Valley dam construction at the Elan Valley. Thanks to Severn Trent Water.

Tony Knight wondered 'if you are aware that they built a small dam in order to supply water to the construction workers that built the whole project. The dam known as the Nant-y-Gro near Rhayader became unused when the main Elan Valley project was finished. It was blown up in July 1942 as part of the experiments being carried out by the Road Research Laboratory on behalf of Barnes Wallis to try and finalise the theory behind his dambusting experiments. They finally established that a contact charge up against the dam wall would do the job and established the amount of explosive that would be required. There is some grainy film still around that shows Wallis climbing up the steep slopes around the dam prior to the explosion.'

In 2004 we celebrated 100 years of the supply of water from the Elan Valley to Birmingham. It is a celebration for fresh water is one of the most precious things in life. It is also a celebration of a magnificent engineering feat and of the belief that the municipality owed a duty to provide its citizens with facilities for their good health irrespective of their wealth.

I thank Mrs J. M. Smith for this photo and for the newspaper cuttings on the opening of the dam.

On Thursday 23 October 1954, Her Majesty the Queen paid her first visit to Wales to open the Claerwen Dam. This photo shows her with Prince Philip, the Duke of Edinburgh, and the Lord Mayor of Birmingham, Alderman W. T. Bowen. Fittingly he was himself a Welshman. The opening of the massive dam culminated the 50 years of water works that have ensured that the people of Birmingham receive a first-class supply of clean, healthy and beautifully soft water.

Behind Claerwen lay a reservoir with a capacity of over 10,000,000,000 gallons, almost the combined capacity of the existing reservoirs, whilst the dam itself contained 700,000 tons of material and boasted a height of 182 feet.

At the ceremony the chairman of the City's Water Committee, Alderman Humphreys, spoke of the time when he had been visited in the early 1920s by Bernard Shaw. On his first morning, Shaw came down to breakfast 'with an expression of satisfaction on his face and remarked, "There is one thing for which you Birmingham people are not sufficiently grateful ... Your water. It must save you thousands of pounds a year in soap.'

Because of the lack of a telephone land line in the vicinity of Elan, news and picture coverage of the event presented difficult problems of communication and the Birmingham Mail employed a number of resources to overcome these difficulties. A team of Norton despatch riders carried reporters' copy from the dam to Llandridod Wells, whilst two radio operators camped on a mountain top in some rough weather to maintain a Very High Frequency link with the New Street office of the Mail so as to pass on photos.

This hi-tech equipment – for the time – was supplemented by carrier pigeons. At 1.35 p.m. ten pigeons were released from Claerwen. Each carried miniature film negatives and less than two hours later they had returned safely to the loft of their owner, George Davies of Court Oak Road, Harborne. Thence they were taken to the Mail's offices in town.

A Hive of Activity: Brum's Gun Quarter

William Hutton, Birmingham's first historian, got it bang on when he wrote that "the ancient and modern state of Birmingham must divide at the reign of Charles the Second. For though she had before held a considerable degree of eminence; yet at that period, the curious arts began to take root, and were cultivated by the hand of genius." Following the English Civil War and the restoration of the monarchy in 1660, Birmingham did indeed begin to transform itself from an important town regionally into a place thrusting itself on to the international stage as one of the world's greatest manufacturing centres.

Why we don't know, but Birmingham's pace of expansion speeded up remarkably. Lists of taxpayers show that in 1671 there were just 69 forges in the town, yet within twelve years this number has expanded greatly to 202. Half of these were packed into Digbeth and Deritend. And in the last 30 years of the seventeenth century, the population also rose spectacularly from about 5,500 to around 15,000.

One of the "curious" trades that was responsible for this outstanding growth was gun making. Its origins are shrouded by a lack of evidence, but the tale is told that in 1692 King William was bemoaning the fact that because guns were not made in England he had to buy them from Holland at "a great expense and a greater difficulty".

Gun Workers in Lancaster Street, about 1912.

In response, Sir Richard Newdigate, a Member of Parliament for Warwickshire, declared that genius resided in the county, and that his constituents could answer his Majesty's wishes. Sir Richard was sent off to Birmingham where he instructed a chap in Digbeth with a pattern for a gun. This "was executed with precision, which, when presented to the royal board, gave entire satisfaction". Orders were immediately issued for large numbers, which were followed by more orders.

By 1798, so great was the production of guns in Birmingham and so important were they to the nation's defence that the government set up viewing rooms at the Tower in Bagot Street, followed in 1812 by the opening of the Proof House in Banbury Street. And as the gun trade waxed it became located in one part of the town – the Gun Quarter.

From the late 1600s landowners began to develop their estates that had hemmed in the built-up area of the town in Digbeth, the Bull Ring, High Street and Deritend. Amongst those who did so was the Weaman family, who layed out the district to the north of Steelhouse Lane (then known as White Hall Lane). Westley's Map of 1731 indicates the emergence of the top ends of Weaman Street and Slaney Street and by Hanson's Map of 1778, the whole of the Gun Quarter was cut through with streets from Snow Hill in the west to Walmer Street (now Lancaster Street) in the east.

The Church of Saint Mary was placed centrally in this area. Built in 1774 in Whittall Street it was on land given by Dorothy and Mary Weaman – hence Weaman Street - and the Lench's Trust, thus Lench Street. Amongst the other streets that were at the core of the new locality were Sand Street, Slaney Street, Price Street, Saint Mary's Row, Catherine Street (later Whittall Street), Walmer Lane (later Lancaster Street), Loveday Street, Steelhouse Lane and the eastern part of Snow Hill.

The presence of manufacturers hereabouts was not disallowed by covenants on the building leases given by the landowners, the Weamans, and gun makers quickly moved in. As early as 1767, according to Sketchley's Directory, there were fourteen gun and pistol makers locally – although the majority of such people, 21 in total, were working elsewhere in the town. Over the ensuing decades, more and more folk involved in gunmaking moved into the neighbourhood and by 1851 in just Weaman Street, 136 residents were in the gun trade.

Some of the masters built large houses that fronted onto a street and in which they and their families lived. Behind their homes, they erected shopping, workshops, and sometimes – for their workers - blind back houses – that is terraces of small dwellings that had no back doors or windows. However, the growing industrial nature of the Quarter soon meant that these better-off masters moved out, and their houses were sub-divided into workrooms.

In common with other neighbourhoods in what became the central area of Birmingham, the Gun Quarter was not developed in one fell swoop. Unlike the large estates laid out by private developers and the council from the 1920s, its growth was patchy and long-drawn out. New streets like Shadwell Street and Princip Street were cut and established streets like Loveday Street were extended so that it was not until the mid-1800s that the area was fully built up.

This photo shows workers at one of the most famous of all Birmingham gunmaking firms, that of W. W. Greener Saint Mary's Row. Elsie Gardner's father, Albert Woodall, worked there for many years and explains that the Row 'ran between Loveday Street and Whittal Street, approximately where the Dental Hospital stands. Greener's made sporting guns of very high quality. I can remember my father telling us of people from the aristocracy coming to be measured for their guns.'

Greener's fame was world-wide and both Brian Stevenson and Brian Henderson recall a western film starring John Wayne in which he tells one of his men 'Go get yu'self a shotgun – a Greener would be best'. Brian Henderson was fortunate enough to be taken by his pal Mick Cox to meet one of the craftsmen at Greener's in 1962. Going down a tunnel entry, the two young men came into a courtyard and entered an old world that soon was to be swept away by redevelopment. Across the end wall ran a wooden stairway. They climbed it and 'we went through a wooden doorway and back in time a hundred years, because Albert Dawe's workshop was from that period.

'I scanned the room from left to right, first the workbench covered with hand files. Albert nodded to us but continued to work at his leg vice. In front of the bench was a cast-iron framed window, the kind with tiny panes of glass. To his right was a wall mounted gun rack, and another across the back wall. Between these, sitting on a low box was a uniformed policeman smoking a cigarette. In the opposite corner was a blazing hearth and gas torch. Next to these were oil and water boshes (tanks).

'Another man hovered for a while, then left saying he would come back. He was waiting for a 'rush job' and may have been there to 'carry' the workpiece to the next craftsman.'

The gun trade was marked by its specialisation and sub-division and Albert epitomised this. He fitted together the gun barrels and stocks and as Brian makes plain, 'it was hand-and-eye work, aligning the stock, perfecting the hinge (making the breech gas-proof), and on the better guns, perfecting the spring ejector, optional for rapid re-loading'.

Howard Essex was a jointer, joining a pair of shotgun barrels to the action and belonged to a highly-respected gunmaking family. His great nephew, John Essex, explains that Howard 'would file the "lumps" underneath the barrels to fit into the action mechanism, fitting the hinge or joint-pin which would allow the barrels to swing down when the gun was 'broken', that is, opened.' The spring between the legs of the vice provided pressure whilst the vice was closed, but 'if the vice were held shut with the hand and the screw undone some way before the hand was released, then the jaws would fly open making a very heavy "clonk" sound. Wilfrid Essex, Howard's brother, had a very raised ridge along the nail of one thumb which was the result of having the thumb caught in such a vice.'

Under Howard's left elbow is his billy for making tea, on the shelf below is a packet of ten 'Wild Woodbines', whilst 'his outdoor clothes hang on the wall; cap, tie, jacket and overcoat. Note that he is wearing collar studs – one under the chin, and one at the back of the neck. Shirts in those days had detachable collars and this would have been removed to keep it clean; no doubt it is under the cap.' I would like to thank John Essex who has provided me with copies of a host of evocative photos and who is also a mine of information about Birmingham's gun trade.

So soon as ever it was established, the Gun Quarter was affected adversely by redevelopment. In the late nineteenth century, the cutting of Corporation Street swept through its outskirts, whilst the building of the General Hospital led to further clearances. Still, Birmingham's Gun Quarter remained a hive of activity because of the myriad of trades associated with gun making. As with their counterparts who fashioned gold and silver, the craftspeople of the Gun Quarter applied their talents to a particular craft and were involved in only part of the process of making guns. It was this marked sub-division of labour that had led gun workers to set up close to each other so that once their own task had been accomplished they could pass on the guns to others.

Today it seems that violent crime has become commonplace and it feels as if gunshots can be heard almost weekly somewhere in Birmingham. Yet fifty years ago and more, at a time when many people endured hardships, young lads could fetch guns from one gun worker to another and walk along the streets of the Gun Quarter without fear of assault.

In fact the Gun Quarter managed to continue as a viable entity and even survived the decline in the gun trade until the 1960s. In that decade, the construction of the Inner Ring Road destroyed much of the district. Thankfully a remnant of streets and old buildings survived, around the 'Bull' and the 'Gunmaker's Arms'. Here a few hardy and talented gunmakers carry on. Perhaps now is the time for the Council to recognise the importance of the Gun Quarter and work with its people to ensure that it will thrive as a distinct and vibrant part of Birmingham.

Showing Off The Goods. Harris and Sheldon

If Birmingham was famed across the world for the quality of its wares, then it was also one of the places where the art of displaying such wares was pioneered. John Cadbury was one of those few people who grasped the significance of showing off goods to their best effect and using such displays to draw people into his shop. Based in Bull Street in the 1820s, his teas and coffees were of the highest standard, but to ensure that shoppers were attracted into his premises he filled his novel and eye-catching plate-glass window with tea chests, tea caddies, cone-shaped sugar loaves, and Chinese vases decorated with flowers and butterflies.

Inside the shop there stood the effigy of a Chinese man dressed exotically and colourfully. He was placed amidst aromatic tea chests and tantalising bags of coffee beans, hops and mustard, and stood besides a long counter upon which the tea was gathered up in a silver scoop before it was weighed on brass scales suspended by lengthy ceiling chains. Mind you, John Cadbury's example was not taken up generally, but fifty-odd years later two young men recognised the importance of the appealing display of goods. They were Sydney Harris and John Sheldon.

Both were prime examples of Brummagem ingenuity, skill, doggedness and sheer graft. In particular, they set themselves the tasks of designing and producing display fittings and then selling them. The pair had met when they were fourteen during their apprenticeships with Alfred Field, a leading export merchant. Working in the Despatch Department they soon realised the importance of export and became especially knowledgeable about Birmingham's many brass products. They must have struck up a strong bond because aged only eighteen they left their employer and within a couple of years they had put together all the money they could pull in and started up in a small place in Crooked Lane. Soon after, by about 1880, they moved to their first factory in Newton Street.

Young Harris and Sheldon successfully focused their energies and expertise in different but complementary areas. Sydney Harris ran production and Joseph Sheldon was in charge of sales. They had no easy job. Shopkeepers may have been skilled in the making and mixing of their goods, but little thought was put into showing those goods off to the best advantage. Instead products were piled higgledy-piggledy into a front window, above which hung a vast oil lamp and from either side which hung string.

Harris and Sheldon set out to transform the look of retailing. They believed that shops would be more alluring, entertaining and profitable places if shopkeepers showed off their goods more cleverly, attractively and temptingly. And they did so, by working up way display fittings an, show-cases, wax figures and architectural metal work. These products were manufactured by a small yet determined and loyal team. It included the Aston brothers and Mr T. Saveker, who later went on to form his own business in sundry shop fittings – a business that continues to thrive.

Determined to succeed, the pair chased their dream and copped hold of it. Within four years of starting up properly in Newton Street they had took over a terrace of cottages and workshops running along Stafford Street to Ryder Street. Over the next few years the business prospered and soon 150 men were employed in the Display Fittings Department, with others in the Joinery Shop. They were joined by the chaps in the Casting Shop, who turned out thousands of glass shelf brackets, sash and other sockets, and the fellers of the Iron Shop, who produced mile after mile of standard and tapped bars.

Like so many great Birmingham firms, Harris and Sheldon made their mark upon the world. Their displays were imported to the United States of America, whilst the German department store of Wertheims in Berlin bought the greater part of their display fittings from Brum. By the early twentieth century, Sydney Harris had retired because of ill health, but his loss did not stop the march forward of the business. It became a public company and opened up offices in London, Manchester, Dublin, Glasgow and Berlin. In addition, strong links were forged with Amsterdam and Rotterdam, and a controlling interest was taken in a South African shopfitting company.

Harris and Sheldon. The shaping and designing of busts.

Joyce Gascoigne joined the company as a junior secretary to the timber buyer in the early 1960s, she was impressed with the ball when 'all expenses were met by the company', and also by the formal dinner and dance held a hotel in London. Joyce stresses that 'it was a very interesting place to work, seeing all the timbers arrive from all over the world. They were involved in fitting out the interior of Rackhams when that was being built and many other large stores such as Selfridges in London and others in Scotland. They had an excellent apprenticeship scheme and the men who worked in the factory took an immense pride in their work and were fine craftsmen.'

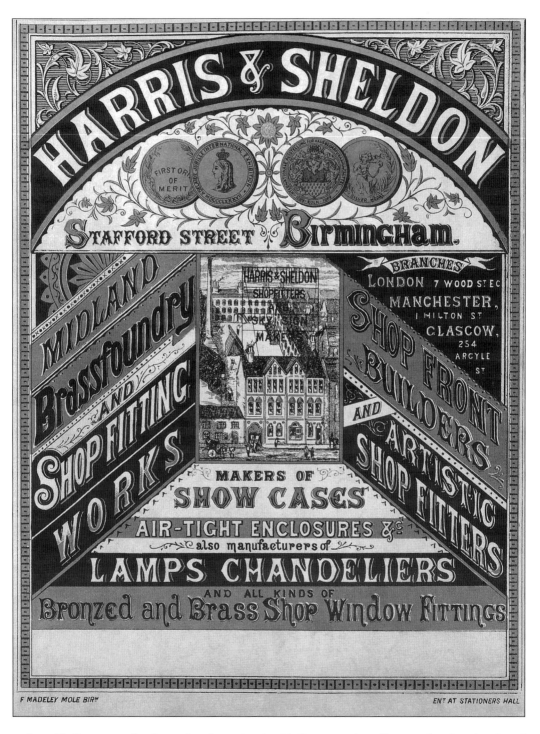

Edna Chillingsworth, the wife of Mr B. G. Chillingworth, tells me that her husband started for the company aged fourteen as an invoice clerk and he earned ten shillings a week. By 1939 he had become works clerk in the maintenance section in Stafford

Street, and thirteen years later through determination, diligence and knowledge of the business Mr Chillingsworth rose to the rank of Company Secretary. He held that position until 1975. Edna Chillingsworth herself joined Harris and Sheldon in December 1941, remaining there as a cashier until her retirement. She recalls well the move from Stafford Street in the city centre to Perry Barr and then, after ten years, to Lord Aylesford's estate at Packington Park in Meriden.

Vanessa Morgan's father, Fred Brinksworth, was another long-serving employee. He started began with company in 1915 and remained until he retired 50 years later. An apprentice shopfitter he 'worked his way up to chief estimator and then contracts manager. He was responsible in the early 1960s for overseeing the shop fitting for the first Woolworth's and M and S stores in Johannesburg and the former Rhodesia. Dad remained very loyal to Harris and Sheldon and loved his time there. As children my brother and I were never short of wooden toys as dad used his skills to provide us with things we wouldn't otherwise have had. The house was filled with handmade furniture and I'm still using the dining suite and dresser.'

This remarkable growth was reflected in the range of products made by Harris and Sheldon. Their catalogues offered about 4,000 items, most of them in six or eight sizes and available in ten finishes – and on top of this a vast array of specials could be worked up. For all the kaleidoscopic array of products and for all the reaching out to a global market, Harris and Sheldon remained true to its base in Birmingham and to it score principles - the need for continual investment in ideas, skills, materials and people.

In the First World War, the company shifted successfully to the making of ammunition boxes, but with the coming of peace Harris and Sheldon returned to the business that it made and that had made it - shop displays. During the tough years of the depression of the 1930s, new and extensive work was gained in fitting out ships, hotels and the big pubs that breweries were now building, and with the onset of war, once again Harris and Sheldon moved successfully into making essential components for aircraft such as the Wellington, Sterling, Lancaster, Spitfire and Beaufighter planes.

Trading conditions after the war were hard, but Harris and Sheldon gained widespread attention in 1950 for the lavish fitting out of the cocktail bar and first-class observation post of the Caronia, one of the Cunard White Star liners. Since then its has continued as a major business based in our region. So the next time the displays in the front window of a store draw you in to gaze at show cases, stands, dummies and architectural metalwork, all illuminated to the best effect, remember - it's all down to Harris and Sheldon.

I am grateful to several people for their help in writing this article. Firstly to the late Mr B. G. Chillingsworth who worked for Harris and Sheldon from 1924 to 1977 and who wrote a history of the company; and secondly to Bill Jordan and Doug Mee for sending me the history and bringing me photographs. All illustrations are courtesy of Harris and Sheldon Group Limited.

War work at Harris and Sheldon.

There must have been something very special about Harris and Sheldon to have inspired so many faithful workers, amongst whom was Les Bamford. His daughter June – who herself was a shorthand typist in the estimating department - tells me that he joined the business as a young lad and finished up as chief estimator. In a reserved occupation during the war, Les worked with the Ministry of Defence on a project to do with tropical packing: 'a big problem was the fact that equipment shipped to the hot and humid Far East was soon becoming unuseable due to the rust. This was eventually solved by incorporating silica gel into the packaging.

'Harris and Sheldon also had a Home Guard company during the war, of which my dad was a member. He not only worked full time during the day but did his stints on night duty as well as attending camp. He also "dug for victory", not only in our back garden but had an allotment as well! June brings to mind 'the lovely dances held at the Grand Hotel. Those were the days when all the ladies wore long ball gowns and were presented with a flower corsage on arrival.'

Strong and Hardy. The Hercules

They used to reckon that in get-up-and-go Brummagem any man Jack could raise himself up from humble beginnings to be a big gaffer if only he had the determination. Brummies praised the self-made man and had little time for those who inherited their wealth. And there were a few who had made a fortune from next to nothing and who were an example to those who wanted to swap their ganseys for fine suits. Not least amongst them were John Taylor, the Brummagem Button King of the 18th century, and John Baskerville, who effected an entire revolution in japanning – whereby goods were made black and glossy by a hard varnish. To this select group could be added Edmund Crane, who created the biggest bicycling factory in the world – the Hercules of Rocky Lane, Aston.

Better known as Ted, he was born a cycling man. His father owned the Petros Cycling Company. When he was 14, just as the twentieth century dawned, Ted went to work in his father's firm. But things weren't going well. The wealthy were forsaking bicycles for the new motor cars and with trade declining, Ted's father was declared bankrupt in 1904. The loss of income swept in a decline of status and a move to a smaller house. In an attempt to improve their financial affairs, Ted's mother operated the business under the direction of her husband and employed her two sons.

Unhappily, the family resorted to a complicated scheme of buying and selling new bikes that lead to serious trouble.

Ted, his brother, Harry, and their father, Edward, were charged and found guilty of Conspiracy to Defraud. Sentenced to between six and ten months hard labour, the Crane men were freed on appeal by a legal technicality. Almost skint, in 1911 the two brothers pooled what little money they had. It came to £25. They rented a back house for six and a tanner a week and Ted then cycled round the streets of Brum, searching out the best bargains for components. In the meantime, Harry used his talents to put together bikes that were reliable, well made and cheap. It was then Ted's task to use his skills to sell the bikes.

Strong of mind and firm of intent, Ted did well at selling what he called "The Hercules". He had chosen the name because of its association with strength and hardiness and he had chosen well. The Hercules was set to make hits mark upon the world.

Orders flowed in so quickly that bigger premises in Conybere Street were taken on and with demand growing significantly; another move was soon made to part of Dunlop's factory in Catherine Street, Aston. In 1914, 10,000 bicycles were made here, but with the onset of the First World War, the Hercules was shifted to munitions work, producing shell plugs.

Reacting swiftly to peace in 1918, Ted Crane believed that there would be a massive demand for bicycles from the working class. He was right, for whilst the rich were driving large cars and the middle class had begun to buy Baby Austins, the workers flocked to purchase a bike that gave them freedom – not only to get to work but also to ride into the countryside for a day out. But with unemployment rising and

Humphrey's Cycle Shop on the Lichfield Road, Aston, taken in the early 1950s. John H Moody recalls well his first bike – a Hercules. As a boy of 13 or 14 in the 1940s it was his pride and joy because before that his bike was made up from old bits and pieces put together by his uncle. This bike was known as ASP – All Spare Parts – and so a new Hercules was a thing of wonder. But he recalls: 'I had only had it a couple of weeks when one day, whilst cycling along Newtown Row, Aston, I got stuck in the tramlines.

'In attempting to jump the bike out of the Tramlines, one side of the front forks broke and I had to dismount. I was living in Kingstanding at the time so it was quite a long way from home and in a bit of a pickle! With a flash of inspiration, I decided to head straight for the Hercules factory. With a face as long as Livery Street I pushed the bike all the way down Park Lane to the factory in Rocky Lane, Aston. I marched through huge gates into the works, no doubt by now looking a bit tearful.

'One of the workmen came over, took the bike off me and sat me down on a packing case. Whilst I sat there he put a new set of front forks on my bike, patted me on the head and sent me on my way a happy, smiling boy again.'

with low wages the norm, working people wanted a bicycle that was cheap and steadfast. The Hercules was that bike. Retailing at £3 19s 9d, it was advertised at "The Best That Money Can Buy At A Price You Can Afford".

In 1921, almost 20,000 bikes were sold and three years later the Cranes bought the rest of Dunlop's factory in Aston. With its main entrance in Rocky Lane, this became one of the most important manufacturing firms in Birmingham. The popular Harry Crane was the more mechanically minded of the brothers and ran the works, but Ted dominated the business.

Refusing to allow trade unions, ready to sack workers if they did not reach his exacting standards and enforcing a strict set of factory rules, Ted Crane was dubbed the "Henry Ford of Cycling" by the workers' paper, the Daily Herald, in 1931. Feared by many, still he paid higher wages than his competitors and was respected by some for his interest in works football and other sporting clubs.

With so many former cycling firms making motor-bikes, Ted Crane's decision to remain with the expanding bicycle trade was inspired. By the 1930s tens of thousands of bikes were made each year and a new factory was now producing many of the components that were needed. The Hercules had become the biggest bicycle manufacturer in the world.

In 1934, Harry Crane died unexpectedly and, now knighted, Ted ran the business alone. As war loomed with Germany, he oversaw munitions work such as the making of mortar bombs, land mines, aircraft ammunition and much more. Like so many Birmingham firms, The Hercules was vital to the war effort.

After 1945, Ted Crane was determined that the Hercules should maintain its unrivalled position, but within a year he had sold the business to Tube Investments, the owners of Raleigh. No longer the gaffer, six months later he resigned from the business. Ted Crane died in 1957 within weeks of TI closing down the Hercules works. A memorial service in St Martin's was attended by hundreds of his former workers. They mourned the loss not only of Ted Crane but also of a great Birmingham manufacturing firm.

Bob Conner kindly sent me this photograph that shows office girls at work at the Hercules factory circa approximately 1921. 'The girl sitting at the front facing the camera and looking at her typewriter is my mother, Louise Richardson - later to become Louise Conner who would have been about 16 at the time. She was born in February 1906 in Small Heath and died in December 1999 at Kings Norton at the age of 93.'

Joan Vickers, the daughter of Ted Crane, has written an insightful account into his life called *Mr Hercules. The Life of Sir Edmund Crane.* This work has been essential in my research for my articles on the Hercules.

Elsie Evans, nee Robinson, has sent in this photo of her and her workmates. She belongs to the famous Robinson family that ran Robbo's Café in Park Lane, Aston for many years. She worked at the Hercules between 1942 and 1953, wheel lacing in the wheel shop. Elsie was great pals with my Auntie Win Martin, nee Wood, who worked nearby at the Midland Wheel in Avenue Road. Elsie is second from the left on the front row. From left top right the others are Gwen, Rose and Lily.

On the back row are Doris Lees, Betty, not known, and Doris's sister, Margaret. It was a real family affair for Doris and Margaret at the Hercules. Their one brother Charles 'Chick Bailey was a clerk there and the other brother, Alfred, was a chargehand storekeeper, who used to put on the shows in the canteen during the dinner break. Chick's wife, Vera, also worked at the Hercules until she left to have a baby, as did Doris's husband after they married. Doris recalls that her foreman was Mr Quinney and after he died he was succeeded by Mr Webb.

Meeting Montgomery: The Met at Washwood Heath

Joseph Wright was a canny and forward-thinking businessman. A leading stage-coach builder and the operator of most of the coaches between London and Birmingham, he quickly realised the coming of railways signalled the end of horse-drawn carriages. He was not downhearted, for swiftly he grasped the opportunity for making carriages for locomotives. In 1844 he patented improvements to four, six and eight-wheeled bogies and soon after he took the big decision to shift his base to Brum. The line to London and the North West had opened fully in 1838 and it was obvious that Birmingham was going to become the centre of England's rail network.

Within three years Wright had taken over another 50 acres and by 1853 he was giving work to 800 talented men. These skilled lads built rolling stock not only for England but also for Egypt, Sweden, India, Australia and a host of other countries. They weren't on their own - the Saltley district was renowned for makers of railway carriages. Down at Adderley Park was Brown and Marshall's. A Brummagem firm, they had also been stage coach makers, based in New Canal Street, and had moved to Saltley in 1853. From their new Britannia Works they designed and crafted the Peninsular and Oriental Express dining cars in 1892.

The Midland Carriage Works in the early 1900s.

Ten years later, the company was amalgamated with Joseph Wright's business, now known as the Metropolitan, and a number of others across the country to form the Metropolitan Amalgamated Railway Carriage and Wagon Company Limited. In 1908, Brown and Marshall's business was transferred to the Saltley Works and its Britannia Works was then sold to the Wolseley Motor Car Company and later the Morris Commercial.

Up the road in Washwood Heath another railway carriage maker remained independent. This was the Midland Railway Carriage and Wagon Company Limited. Formed in Birmingham about 1844, initially it supplied to coal owners and others railway wagons that it had bought. Then in 1864 then Midland began manufacturing itself. Quickly, the business pioneered wagon leasing and the hire purchase of wagons. Thirty years later, it bought 62 acres of land from Lord Norton off Leigh Road, Washwood Heath.

In 1919, the Midland was bought by Cammell Laird and ten years later joined the great combine of the Metropolitan-Cammell Carriage and Wagon Works, which included Joseph Wright's old firm. During the Second World War, the Met as a whole became the biggest supplier of fighting tanks in the country, building a greater variety of tanks than elsewhere. Many of these ingenious tanks were used successfully in the D Day landings in Normandy and in crossing the Rhine. The Met was also a major supplier of radar mechanical equipment, producing many such vehicles at Saltley.

Mr W. H James has sent in this photo of the retirement of his father, the late Mr William H James, from the Metropolitan Cammell railway carriage company in Washwood Heath. A father of seven, William worked at the Met for 40 years or more and when he left the firm gave him a portable radio amongst other things.

His son writes, 'When he first started there he was unloading sheet metal with some other men when some of the metal sheets started to fall and my father saved one of the workers from being crushed to death by pushing him out of the way. But my father got caught himself and ended up in hospital with a broken leg.

'He was offered compensation from his factory of having a light job so he became an overhead crane driver as work was hard to come by. In those days there were a lot of men on the treacle stick (unemployed). He was one of the best fathers you could ever have. God bless him, he's no longer with us now, only in spirit, and I miss him a lot.'

The workers of the Met stood foursquare in the battle for our freedom but sadly that counted for nothing in 2004 when the last of the workers there were laid off. Despite a strong order book and success at making the Pendolino tilting carriages for Virgin Trains and despite a massive public protest, the French owners of the Met, Alstom, closed down these historic works. I dedicate this article to the workers, with whom I was proud to join in a protest march in Paris against the closure.

Irene Evans is the worker meeting General Montgomery in this photo. Irene worked in the machine shop at the Met 'first on a drilling machine and then on a lathe. After a while I was promoted and worked on a large USA capstan. My job was doing the inside of the tank wheels. We were given Dutch clogs because the swarf used to cut our feet. I used to try and sing for the night workers, singing The White Cliffs of Dover, and hope for the best.

'My Mom worked at the Met on a large heavy overhead crane to lift the tanks from one end of the bay to the other, and dad worked there and my sister. One day the director came round and I wondered what I had done wrong. My foreman came back to me and said, 'You have been chosen to meet Montgomery. You will have new overalls to wear, a new turban and some make-up on.'

'I used to go up to the Met club a lot dancing and met my husband Dennis there. He served at El Alemain in the 8th Army. We married in 1947 still working at the Met.

Dennis had his service watch for 30 years and finished up doing 40 years. Our son Donald was also down the Met and had his 26 years watch.'

On leaving school at fourteen in 1942, Ken Morris 'had already secured a job with the now defunct Birmingham Gazette as a 'copy boy' when I had a directive from the Ministry of Labour under War-time rules that I must contribute to the War Effort and I was directed to report to the "Met" in Common Lane, Washwood Heath. Catching the tram from the Fox & Goose at 7.30 each morning, Saturday included, a walk down Common Lane and I was plunged into an industrial world.

'My first job was in oxyacetylene cutting of armour plating for "Valentine" tanks. I worked in what was the longest, biggest manufacturing shop in the Midlands known as the "Avenue", which had been used for building train carriages. A Mr Morse was the manager with foreman Mr Scott and under foreman Mr Newey.

'All manner of people had been directed to work there including conscientious objectors. Tommy Pardoe, the Birmingham Boxer, worked there and an amateur boxer, Arthur Wright, known as "Bowie Wright" who ran the Met Boxing Club of which I was a member. I graduated as a fitter and used to install map cases, shell racks, tank commander fittings in the turrets of Valentine tanks, Sherman tanks and Cromwell tanks. Many was the time my friend Ron and I used to climb into the tank's turrets and tune in the tank commander's radio to listen to "workers playtime".

'The Amphibian tanks you mention were known as Duplex Drive and had a waterproof canvas screen of about 3,5 metres, which was erected by cylinders, at intervals n the tanks, which were activated by air pressure; they had two propellers. There were Canadian soldiers seconded to the Met who tested these tanks on completion, by driving along Washwood Heath Road, Coleshill Rd, Chester Rd and on to Sutton Park, where they were tested for floatation etc in one of the Sutton Park pools. One day I was welding shell racks for gun limbers when an entourage of management and military were touring the factory and bending over my work I felt a touch on my shoulder and General Bernard Montgomery asked me if I enjoyed my job and commended me for helping the War effort. He had come to view the Sherman Duplex Drive Tanks prior to the D Day invasion.

'Beneath the Met at Common Lane were cellars and a rail line which ran all the way to the Met at Saltley. There was also a Home Guard practice rifle range, which must have been at least 300 yards long. On the morning of D Day, 6 June, almost the entire workforce went outside to watch the glider and hordes of aircraft en route to France.

'The Met had a super sports ground near the Fox & Goose pub in Coleshill Road, Ward End, and were leading lights in works league football, along with Latch & Batchelor, Fisher's, Tangye's, B'ham City Police, Hamstead Colliery and many other local works teams. A happy time at the Met was brought to an end when I was called up at the age of 18 and found myself serving in the Middle East. On Demobilisation I rejoined the Met and found myself building buses for home and overseas at the works in Bickenhill Lane, Marston Green. It was with a heavy heart I finally left the Met and joined Joseph Lucas.'

The Model Brewery. Smith's

Famed for our fashioners of metal and for the manner in which our people could take a lump of metal and style it into a thing of beauty desired across the world, yet Birmingham was a town where a host of other trades also flourished in the nineteenth century. None more so than breweries. Today there is no major brewery in Birmingham. What a contrast that is with the situation in the 1870s when over 90% of public houses and beer houses had a licence to brew beer. Amongst them were the celebrated Bellefield Inn, Winson Green recently closed, the Wellington in Gooch Street and the Wagon and Horses, still open thankfully in Adderley Street.

By the 1880s, the rapid decline of the publican brewer had set in but brewing itself was not dropping off. Indeed it was expanding as common brewers began to sell their beer to the licensed trade. And as they did so, they began to buy up as many premises as they could in which they could supply their own ales. Amongst the great breweries of later nineteenth-century Brum was Holt's. Belonging to the Fulford family, whose members had been involved in brewing and malting since 1819, the concern had 155 pubs and beer houses by 1890. Ansell's was also making its mark, and it too had started out as a malster's and also as a hop merchant's. And then there was Smith's Brewery.

Like its bigger rivals, Smith's traced its origins deep into Birmingham's history, to a Thomas Smith who was a master cooper. In fact, Thomas was mentioned as one of only nine coopers in Birmingham in the second Directory of trades of our town that was compiled in 1776. Working from 70, Dale End he had a fine reputation for crafting oaken vats, mash tuns, casks and fermenting vessels, and his business was carried on after his death by his son William.

Born in 1819 in Pinfold Street, William began the family's move into brewing. In 1846 he took on the lease of a house at 24, Aston Road, just up from Holte Street and Love Lane and next door to what became 'The General Wolfe. In the extensive out buildings of his new home he carried on as a cooper. But seven years later William successfully applied for a licence to brew and sell beer and changed his premises into 'The Model'. The new brewer cum publican fast gained a reputation for the quality of his beer as much as for that of his casks, and within two years he decided to make additions to his brewery and plant so that he might add wholesale brewing to his operation.

A pioneer in the business of selling beer to other publicans, William made rapid progress in his new field. In 1860, spurred on by doing so well, he bought two acres of land in Queens Road, Aston and upon it he built the 'Queen's Hotel'. Unlike 'The Model', the new place had a full licence and was able to sell wine and spirits as well as beer. Running the two premises, William must have gradually realised that his future lay with his new venture just across the Aston Brook and in the developing town of Aston. Within a couple of three years of opening the 'Queen's' he had added a malt house and this was followed by the construction of a large cellarage. Then in 1865, the whole of his brewing concern was moved from Gosta Green to the new Model Brewery in Queens Road.

William became a wealthy man but after his death in 1878 t seemed that his business might disappear with him, for William left behind not only a widow and two children but also six children from a previous marriage. To provide for his dependents, William's brewery and maltings were sold, along with the Queen's Hotel adjoining them and all his other properties. Thomas and Henry Smith, two of William's oldest sons, each bought one of their father's pubs, but the Model Brewery itself was purchased by the

Workers at Smith's Model Brewery, Aston. I thank Betty Cox, nee Weston, for these photos and for her help in putting together this article. Betty worked for Smith's for ten years from 1947. It was a very busy but happy period of her working life. As secretary to Mr Page, the surveyor, she worked from 8.30 until 5.30 Mondays to Fridays and from 8.30 till 1 o'clock on Saturdays. She and three other secretaries operated in a small office above the cellars where the spirits were bottled.

One job that Betty loved doing was after the auditors had been 'the Profit and Loss sheets had to be typed and I always did them on a long typewriter carriage', and she recalls that in and around the offices everyone was called by their surnames.

Betty worked with Miss Wawen, Miss O'Driscoll and Miss Smith, who made her wedding dress for her in 1950. When the brewery finally closed, Betty and Mr Wood, the company secretary, were the last staff to leave, having to clear up the remaining paperwork.

Atkinson brothers. It was here that Frederick Smith, the youngest son of the first marriage, served his time - and it was to be Frederick who relaunched the Smiths back into brewing.

Frederick had worked with his father in the business and after two years with Atkinson's he made himself independent by buying the Victoria Brewery, just down the road from The Model Brewery, on the Lichfield Road in Aston. He began his new venture on 18 August 1880 and renamed it The Aston Model Brewery. A young man who had just reached 21, Frederick must have been determined of spirit, hard-working and cute of mind. Within eight years, his endeavours led to an expansion whereby he took the lease of 6,000 square yards of land on the Lichfield Road, upon which built a new and bigger brewery.

Sir Frederick Smith.

Each year, it seemed that the ambitious and successful Frederick was able to improve his premises and move his business forward: in 1890 he had built new offices and a home; two years later a sixty-quarter malt house was put up; and in 1895 the firm became a limited company. The same year, Smith's bought a significant number of pubs and to cope with the increased output of beer needed for the new outlets, a new wing to the brewery was added between 1898 and 1900, along with a bottling department and new casking washing sheds.

Unlike some successful businessmen who wished their sons to become landed gentlemen, Frederick was keen that his offspring should be part of his operations. His elder son, Frederick, studied at the Brewing School of The University of Birmingham and brought his expertise into the firm, whilst the younger son, Sydney, became responsible for the brewery's tied houses. Both men served in the First World War and with the return of peace, their attentions turned to further improvements. In 1922 the interior of the brewery was remodelled, new plant was brought in and a fresh artesian well was sunk to fetch up more supplies of the pure Aston water so noted for the brewing of beer and vinegar.

Seven years later, George V knighted Frederick Smith for his services to the communities of Aston and Birmingham. His business continued until 1957 when it was bought out by Butler's of Wolverhampton.

Thanks to Mike James who states that the 'photograph is a brewery outing from Smith's Brewery, Aston. The location is Solihull Station. My Father is on the extreme right with Albert Mitchener immediately next to and slightly behind him. This must have been mid 1930s.'

Burning Bright: The Valor

At the dawn of the eighteenth century coal-gas lighting had been gifted to the world by William Murdock, a Birmingham-based Scot who was vital to the success of Matthew Boulton and James Watt. For all that remarkable achievement, gas lights in the home were rare for generations. As the twentieth century beckoned, it was still candles and paraffin lamps that lit up houses across the city – and it was the selling of paraffin for that purpose that had set Joe Lucas on the path to industrial greatness.

He'd traipsed the streets, flogging paraffin from a bucket to householders, and then as trade picked up he bought himself a basket carriage to hold his wares, which he sold to paraffin shops and the like. Soon after he went on to buy the patent for a ship's paraffin lamp, the Tom Bowling lamp, and that led him into making lamps for bicycles. From that beginning of a hawker on the streets of Brum emerged one of the world's greatest electrical engineering concerns.

But Old Joe was not the only one who created a celebrated firm from the oil business. So too did Arthur Wilson-Browne. His father was a merchant in Birmingham and he had a sharp eye for a trading opportunity. Oil was essential not only for lighting a house but also for lubricating machinery. To satisfy that demand a new firm called the Anglo-American Company (later known as Esso) was fetching increasing supplies of oil into Britain. But there was a problem. The company needed suitable storage containers. Wilson-Browne senior became aware of this need and stepped in to address it.

In 1890, he took over a small shop in Ludgate Hill – now deep in Birmingham's financial district but then an area of housing and workshops. Here he set up his two sons to make the necessary containers, after examining models of oil storage cabinets and tanks from the United States of America. The one son Percy soon fanaiged, but young Arthur proved to be persevering, resilient, determined and skilled. With just one adult worker and a young lad, Arthur made his storage units by hand from sheet metal. His father had also taken over a small firm and its symbol became invaluable: it was a shield with the word Valor written across it diagonally. This was the origins of the Valor Company Limited which later became famous as Valor Heating of Wood Lane, Erdington.

Things went well and more room was needed. At first Arthur rented rooms over his shop but then he moved nearby to Church Street, where he took over an old public house, a malt house and a couple of small houses. It was a typical Brummie workshop. There were few purpose-built factories in the city. Most manufacturing premises grew up haphazardly and higgledy-piggledy, beginning in 'shopping', workshops, and expanding to take over adjoining dwellings, shops and other buildings.

What's more Arthur and his father exemplified another Birmingham characteristic: the connection between commerce and manufacturing and the interchange between the two sectors. By 1896, production at the Valor had increased so much that a gas engine was needed to provide power and the company was making a wide range of oil storage units, from six gallon to 50 gallon capacity. Other products included shop oil tanks with hinged covers and taps, carbide storage tanks, oil filters and the 'Patent Dripless Oil Drum'. Petrol cans were also a feature of output. One hundred a week were made, indicating the growth of motoring and its positive impact upon the economy of our city. And again, like so many Birmingham manufacturers, Arthur was keen to diversify and move into new fields of production. Attracted by the bicycling boom, he began to make bikes. But a slump hit the bicycle trade in the early 1900s and production was ceased. The downturn in trade badly affected others, including a company called Arrow Cycle of Aston Cross which closed down. Keen to have better premises Arthur took over the Arrow Works.

He soon introduced the making of fire extinguishers – a ware which became deeply associated with the Valor. Brass fittings were vital to this new product and they were supplied by the nearby Aston Brass Ltd, which finally was taken over by the Valor in 1932 Another new product was also to become inextricably linked with the name of Valor – a portable oil heater known as the Perfection. This was an American design and at first the Valor imported the parts from the USA and assembled them at Aston Cross.

As with so many Birmingham firms, the coming of the First World War saw a rapid and effective shift to war work. The Valor's oil containers, petrol cans, fire extinguishers and portable oil heaters were essential goods. After the war, demand continued to rise for the oil heaters in particular and this led to a change of ownership of the firm.

Early days at Valor.

The Perfection oil heater and another called the Reform were marketed in Britain by the Anglo-American Company, for which Valor supplied the storage tanks. With a growing bond between the two companies, F. E. Powell, the chairman of the big American business resolved to take over the Birmingham firm. He did in 1919. Arthur Wilson-Browne stayed on as chairman, but the board was packed with Anglo-American people, including Powell himself.

Powell dropped the name Perfection and replaced it with that of Valor. Driven ahead by his ambitious plans, in 1924 the company bought 24 acres of land in Erdington to facilitate the mass production of oil heaters. The main factory building was of a great size: 580 feet long and 360 feet wide and was reputed to be covered by the largest roof in Birmingham. Another large unit was built next door for Aston Brass.

By early 1926, the extensive and impressive new factory was ready for workers to begin the task of making the Valor an international name – and within a short time they achieved the objective set them of turning out 1,000 oil heaters a day. Crucially, the heaters were no longer made of American parts. Instead they were a British product called the 525. In effect the 525 was the same as the Perfection. An innovative and efficient heater, and bar for a few changes, the 525 continued to be produced on the same lines until after the Second World War. Even with improvements, the post-war model looked similar to that which had left Aston Cross in 1902.

Making 525 oil heaters.

At the same time, the output of petrol cans soared. Ten thousand were made on each shift and there were two shifts a day. Mind you there were problems facing that market. Garages were becoming more common and many motorists were beginning to buy their petrol from such places rather have it stored in their own cans. But the Valor was well placed to cope with this changing pattern of consumption, for it also supplied suitable petrol tanks for forecourts.

So successful were Valor's products that the factory had to be extended within six months of opening - and by the outbreak of the Second World War it occupied thirteen acres, whilst there were another 30 acres in reserve, and it gave work to more than one thousand men and women. Each year, hundreds of thousands of products poured out of the works. Again, like so many other major Birmingham manufacturing concerns, the Valor was almost a self-contained set up. Amongst other sections, it boasted a tool room, lacquering and dipping shops, wick department, assembly sections, nickel plating, japanning and bonderising plant, a modern brassfoundry, and shops for hot stamping, polishing and machines.

Importantly, the Valor did not rest upon its laurels as the market leader. It had a research department where new ideas were developed and models were tested so that Valor products stayed up to date with the progress of the application of oil. Unlike, most Birmingham firms the workers did not go in on a Saturday morning but worked a five-day week. Each morning and afternoon there was a tea break. Like the long weekend, this was viewed by management not only as a good thing for employees but as a means for increasing production. Moreover, the workers had the facilities of a seventeen acre playing ground and clubs for football, bowls, tennis and other sports. The issue of happy workers was an important one, and the Valor also provided a canteen – which became a place of entertainment after work.

Proudly the company proclaimed that all the material it used was of British manufacture and was made to a rigorous specification. This was enabled by an Inspection Department that operated from the entry of raw materials to the exit of the finished product. But the Valor's expansion was not without its setbacks. In the winter of 1927/8 it took on and saw off a cheaper foreign import that challenged the 525. Advertised with the slogan 'Cosy warmth for less than 1d per hour', in the Depression that soon followed this oil heater became a vital source of cheap fuel for poor families as much as it was a convenient product for the better off.

Because of changes in American laws, by the end of the 1930s the Valor had become an independent, British-owned company – although its bond with Anglo-American remained powerful. In effect, Valor continued to make the goods whilst Anglo-American sold them. As it had done in 1914, the company swiftly shifted to war production in 1939. The 525 was used by all the armed services and in air raid shelters, whilst workers also made four and half million petrol cans; almost a million minefield markers; nearly three million ammunition boxes; and a host of other essential wares such as smoke generators, demolition mines, storage shelves, cordite reels and drinking water tanks.

The building of the Wood Lane factory, Erdington.

At the same time, the associated company of Aston Brass made stirrup pumps, that vital tool for fighting fires in the Blitz. Bombed once on its vitreous enamel shop, production was unaffected and with the coming of peace, the Valor once more reached out to the domestic market.

The ending of the Second World War brought austerity and not prosperity. Rationing continued and shortages abounded. In these difficult economic conditions, many firms found it hard. The Valor bucked the trend. Even though its famed 525 oil heaters were selling in great numbers, its designers fastened upon the principle of innovation and in 1948 they came up with the No. 11 Convector Heater.

The first of its kind, it brought together modern design and technological developments. Alert to the weariness of the British people with utility wares, the designers at the Valor made the No. 11 Convector Heater rectangular in shape and stylish. They also brought in crucial technical improvements. The new heater had a larger fount, allowing it to burn for more than 24 hours without refuelling, and its blue flame burner did away with odours. More and more middle-class couples were doing away with servants. Instead they were buying labour-saving devices for the housewife and the No. 11 Convector fitted the bill because it required less cleaning and re-filling. The heater was launched officially in November 1949. It was a spectacular success and from 1951 it was taking Esso Blue paraffin, reflecting the change of name of the Anglo-American Company to the Esso Petroleum Company.

As the 'Never had it so good days' of the late 1950s dawned, more and more people bought Valor heaters to warm their homes. That demand was further stimulated by cold winters and threats to coal production. In the winter of 1956-7 an amazing two million oil heaters were sold, many of them made by Valor, but two years later sales slumped. Drawn in by a buoyant market, newcomers began to make oil heaters and hit Valor's sales, and then a terrible fire caused by an oil heater – not a Valor - filled the newspapers with negative publicity. Sales dropped off drastically as the public turned away from oil heaters and began to buy electric and gas heaters.

With 90% of its production focused on portable oil heaters, Valor was hit badly and in 1960 output was cut back significantly and workers were laid off. Seeking to regain the public's confidence, Valor was involved in originating a new British Standard specification. Sales picked up slowly, but they were never going to reach the massive figures of the boom years. In these circumstances the company had to diversify or die.

A metal ironing board manufacturer was bought and production was moved to Wood Lane, whilst it was decided to end the agreement whereby Esso had the agency in the United Kingdom to distribute Valor products – although the oil heaters continued to recommend customers to buy Esso Blue. Then in 1962 Valor took over an electrical heating company which made garden equipment for the summer market, and an export drive was launched. By the end of 1963, Valor was also involved in oil and gas-fired central heating and the number of employees had more than doubled from 650 to 1,750.

Led by the determined Michael Montague, Valor moved on to purchase a group supplying fittings for cisterns and plumbers and solid fuel appliances. Now covering all aspects of heating, Valor diversified into plastic cisterns, which became a major part of the business. By the late 1960s, the Valor was a large, successful and dynamic group of companies with three main divisions: heating appliances; builders' supplies; and general hardware.

Since then there have been far-reaching changes. By the end of the twentieth century, Valor fires were owned by Newmond Plc, and in November 2000 that company joined Baxi Heating. Today the Valor Wood Lane site is the headquarters of Baxi Fires Division (United Kingdom).

For their vital input into the research of this article I should like to thank and acknowledge David Acock, Paddy Fletcher and Brenda Elt, who wrote to me in 2001 on behalf of the Valor Consultative Committee of Managers, Staff and Factory Workers Representatives. This article could not have been written without that input.

Chapter 4:
Sights, Sounds and Smells of Old Brum

Holly, Ivy and Lanterns. A Traditional Christmas

Holly and ivy, lanterns and stagecoaches, the singing of carols and the giving of presents, plum pudding and mulled wine, Christmas trees and Christmas cards, yule logs and mistletoe, snow and Father Christmas, goodwill to all men and family gatherings - all of these come to mind when we think of a traditional Christmas. And one man's name jumps to the fore when we conjure up that proper Christmas, a Christmas like they had in the old days. It is, of course, Charles Dickens.

With his Christmas scenes in *Pickwick Papers* (1836) and then *A Christmas Carol*, Dickens has had a profound effect on the way we celebrate Christmas. But Dickens was not alone in bringing to us a vision of the way the festival was carried on in days gone by. Another writer had just as great an influence in his homeland of America. His name was Washington Irving and he is connected deeply with Birmingham.

Born in New York City, Washington Irving came to England after the Napoleonic Wars and set up in business in Liverpool. Unfortunately, the venture failed and downhearted as to his future he decided to visit his sister, Sarah, and her husband

This is a rare and early photograph of Aston Hall, probably taken in the 1870s by a J. Rollason. Aston Hall was probably the inspiration for Bracebridge Hall in Washington Irving's Old Christmas.

Washington Street in 1964. Named after the author Washington Irving, this picture was taken just before the street was cleared in the late 1950s.

Henry Van Wart. Descended from Dutch settlers who had helped to found New Amsterdam - later New York - Van Wart was a major figure in Birmingham and it was at his house on the corner of Frederick Street and Graham Street, Hockley that Washington Irving recovered his spirits and set his life upon a successful path when he wrote *Rip Van Winkle*.

This story formed part of the *Sketch Book*, as did *The Tales of Sleepy Hollow* - also written in Hockley - and *Old Christmas*. This last story was crucial in the pushing forward to Americans the idea of an olde English Christmas and it focuses upon Bracebridge Hall. It is most likely that Aston Hall and its grounds, then part of a great estate, were the inspiration for Bracebridge Hall - and let us not forget that the last of the Holtes, the ancient owners of the Hall, was a Mary who was married to Abraham Bracebridge, after whom is called Bracebridge Street, Aston.

In *Old Christmas*, an American traveller chances upon an old acquaintance, Frank Bracebridge, who invites the visitor to share old English hospitality with his father, 'The Squire'. The two men arrive in a coach, from which they alight so as to walk unto the hall. Their road 'wound through a noble avenue of trees, among the naked branches of which the moon glittered as she rolled through the deep vault of a cloudless sky. The lawn beyond was sheeted with a slight covering of snow, which here and there sparkled as the moonbeams caught a frosty crystal; and at a distance might be seen a thin, transparent vapour, stealing up from the low grounds, and threatening gradually to enshroud the landscape.'

The sound of music came from the servants' rooms in the family mansion, 'where a great deal of revelry was permitted, and even encouraged by the Squire throughout the twelve days of Christmas, provided everything was done comformably to ancient usage. Here were kept up the old games of hoodman blind, shoe the wild mare, hot cockles, steal the white loaf, bob apple and snapdragon. The Yule Log and Christmas candle were regularly burnt, and the mistletoe, with its white berries, hung up to the imminent peril of all the pretty handmaids.'

A wonderful photo of the Co-op in High Street, Birmingham, all done up for Christmas.

As the Christmas unfolded, so too did Washington Irving expand upon his theme of a traditional English Christmas. Whether or not such a thing has ever existed, it is real enough in our minds and in our thoughts. We all want such a festival, like it was in the old days - but without Washington Irving as much as Charles Dickens we would not even know what a traditional Christmas should be. So when you pass Washington Street and Irving Street, or when you're down along Frederick Street and Graham Street, or when you're wandering around Aston Hall just think how Washington Irving's stay in Brum has affected our ideas as to how we should celebrate the greatest of our festivals.

So let us hark back to The Old Christmas of days of yore when Christmas dinner was served in Bracebridge Hall:

> Lo, now is come the joyful'st feast!
> Let every man be jolly,
> Eache room with yvie leaves is drest,
> And every post with holly.
> Now all our neighbours' chimneys smoke,
> And Christmas blocks are burning;
> Their ovens they with bak't meats choke,
> And all their spits are turning.
> Without the door let sorrow lie,
> And if, for cold, it hap to die,
> We'll bury't in a Christmas pye,
> And evermore be merry.'

Church of hope. Church of The Messiah

It may have been the first day of the New Year but many Brummies, that Wednesday 1 January 1862 didn't promise hope – it was yet another tough day in the midst of yet another hard winter. Bare-footed kids traipsed the streets, holding out their hands for the sympathy of the better-off and hoping for a ha'penny that'd buy them a piece. Out of collar blokes in ragged clothes lined up for soup doled out at kitchens set up by good-hearted shopkeepers. And women with shawls pulled fast around their shoulders clutched the odd possession they still owned and queued doggedly outside the pawn shop.

There was nothing out of the ordinary in such schemes. Each year the poor dreaded the onset of General Winter, fearful of his heavy tread and frit of his harsh touch. It was a struggle to welcome the new year when it promised so little and when all it signalled was more weeks of scratting to survive, more days of being clammed through too little food and more parky days without any fuel. Yet for one group of citizens 1 January 1862 was momentous for it was the day on which the Unitarians opened their new place of worship –the Church of the Messiah in Broad Street.

A Non-Conformist group with no set doctrines; the Unitarians were small in numbers yet powerful in their influence. One of the early members of their congregation had been Joseph Priestley; the famed scientist who had lived at a house called Fair Hill in Sparkbrook. And now, in the mid years of the nineteenth century, they included a number of prominent local families. There were the Martineaus, who were involved in the professions as well as in manufacturing and one of whom had recently been a mayor of Birmingham. There were the Nettlefolds, who owned a major screwmaking business locally. There were the Kenricks, who ran the world famous firm which made hollow ware. And there were the Beales – who also boasted a former mayor – the Phipsons and the Rylands.

That first of January these and other wealthy families stepped into their carriages, left their Edgbaston homes and made their way along the Hagley Road across Five Ways and down Broad Street. Their destination was probably the most curiously located church in the whole of Birmingham. Built on the corner of St Peter's Place and almost opposite Gas Street, it lay across the Birmingham and Worcester Canal. No wonder it had such great, sturdy arches – for without them the church could never have spanned the cut.

Designed by J. J. Bateman in the Gothic style, it had an equally impressive entrance with three arches held up by granite columns and above which was an eye-drawing window. But most notable of all the church's features was an elegant spire which rose up 150 feet. Costing the huge sum of £10,000 and having room for 1,000 worshippers, the new chapel replaced the New Meeting House in Moor Street – which was bought by the Catholics and was renamed St Michael's. Immediately the Church of the Messiah became a notable Birmingham landmark, but within a few years it had also emerged as a focal point of the struggle to transform Brum into the best-governed city in the world.

Left: Barefoot children in Birmingham in the late 1800s. Right: Despite the actions of the preachers and worshippers at the Church of the Messiah and elsewhere, tens of thousands of young Brummies continued to live in dreadful conditions – as shown by this photograph of Hanley Street in the 1920s. Thanks to Sylvia Leigh.

In 1869 Dr H W Crosskey was appointed minister and it was his preaching which made his church a lode star for reformers. He urged the members of his congregation to propel themselves into politics and use their position and prestige for the good of their fellow men and women. He wasn't on his own in pushing forward a message of Christian action and involvement in the wider world. At the Church of the Saviour in Edward Street, the charismatic George Dawson was another who declared that the better-off owed a duty to those who were less fortunate. Whilst this civic gospel was also exclaimed by Charles Vince at the Baptist Mount Zion Chapel in Graham Street and by Robert Dale, the pastor of Carr's Lane Congregational Church.

Their message was heeded, none more so than by Joseph Chamberlain. In the 1870s he and his supporters wrested control of the council from the tight grip of the economists – those who wished the corporation to spend as little money as possible and who saw little need to act to help the position of the poor. In a few years the Chamberlainites made plain the wrongness of such an approach. They took over for the corporation the privately-owned gas and water companies and brought clean water and light to the furthest yard. Most wonderfully such initiatives increased healthiness and lowered death rates.

The Church of the Messiah is on the right in this shot of Broad Street in the 1950s.

Bare-footed and ragged children could still be seen on the streets of Brum for many years – but the actions of the men and women who belonged to the Church of the Messiah did make a difference. They strove for the well being of the many and though their church may have disappeared, their example should not be forgotten.

Tragedy in Villa Street. Flooding of Hockley Brook

The air was heavy and no moon was visible on 14 July 1923. It seemed like just another clammy summer's night when you had to keep all the windows open to try and get a bit of air moving about. But all of a sudden, the air really shifted as great streaks of lightning slashed across the sky and as powerful claps of thunder rent apart the silence. Quickly, the thunder and lightning was followed by rain belting down so hard that the drops bounced off the pavement. Anyone who was out and about was drenched and swiftly took shelter, thinking the storm would soon blow itself out. But it didn't. The rain seemed to be throwing itself at the streets and buildings of Brum and it wasn't long before water was gushing out of the suffs as if they were springs, whilst brooks which were hidden beneath the ground burst free of their culverts and transformed horse roads into fast-flowing streams.

Across the city, low-lying districts were flooded. In Sparkbrook, the Spark turned the Stoney Lane and parts of the Stratford Road and Highgate Road into a whirling lake, and in Digbeth, Deritend and sections of Nechells, the River Rea rose up and overwhelmed the streets. But it was Hockley that took the worst pasting as the Hockley Brook was transformed from a placid stream to a furious flow which surged into the roads across which it ran.

Four houses in Villa Street had been shored up after a previous flood and now they collapsed under the pressure of the water. As the bricks and mortar fell, the impact forced a huge wave to thrust itself down the street. One old lady was carried to safety by a policeman who risked his life to struggle against the ripping currents that came up nearly to his shoulders. Nearby in Hunter's Vale, Mr Mathewson, his mother and a teenage relative were inside a house against which ten feet of water was pounding. They had with them Mrs Robinson and her seven-year old daughter. All of them had to be rescued by firemen and police officers. In total, fifty-odd people had to be saved and were looked after at the Dispensary in Farm Street before they were taken to sleep on the floor of Saint Saviour's Mission.

It was one of the worst floods in the recorded history of the Hockley Brook, but thankfully such disasters were soon to be averted through the Hockley Brook Improvement Scheme. Until 1911, the Hockley Brook divided Birmingham from Handsworth, then in Staffordshire, and Aston, Warwickshire. In that year both these places became part of Birmingham, but the brook continued to be of significance as a Parliamentary boundary.

The stream itself used to run openly eastwards from Rabone Lane by the Smethwick Gas Works, up alongside Ninevah Road over Factory Road and parallel with South Road, Handsworth. It crossed into Hockley at the bottom of Soho Hill and Hockley Hill and went with Farm Street, going over Hunters Vale, Villa Street, Wellesley Street, and Burbury Street in Hockley, and then across Berners Street, Wilton Street, Wheeler Street, Lennox Street and Guildford Street in Lozells.

Pumping out the water from the flooded cellar of the New Inns on the corner of Hunters Vale.

Joseph Scott was in his eighties when he wrote to me and he recalled that in either this storm or another, three boys were sitting on the wall of the bridge in Villa Street when it collapsed. There was also flooding in Icknield Street where the pavement dipped opposite Norton's. Doris Bott was born in 1919 and lived opposite the 'Brook Tavern' in Lennox Street, Lozells. She remembers that she was four or five when 'they came and dug up the road to widen the brook, but unfortunately it wasn't where they'd dug'. Doris also recollects that 'they used to say that the houses in Hunters Vale used to get flooded when we had a storm'.

Len Osborne also has unhappy memories of the flooding. When he was 'a boy of about 12 years old, in the 1920s, I lived in Church Street, Lozells, the next street was Villa Street. One day we had a torrential thunderstorm, all Villa Street and Hunters Vale were flooded; a small river. The Hockley Brook ran through Villa Street, at one place there was a 6ft wall which ran alongside the river. Four or five youths climbed the wall, my brother who was older than I wanted to climb the wall too but could not manage it. The pressure of water caused the wall to collapse, two youths jumped clear, a brave policeman jumped in and saved one youth, the others were sucked under Villa Street and found the next day in a tunnel under Aston Brook Street, two or three miles away. A sad day for Villa Street; just a reminder of my boyhood days.'

Because that district used to be part of Aston Manor Urban District Council, the Hockley Brook then becomes known as the Aston Brook. From Wheeler Street, it cuts across Porchester Street, Alma Street and the bottom end of High Street, Aston. Thence it flows between Phillips Street and Aston Brook Street, crosses over the Aston Road North and goes behind Whitehouse Street and across Chester Street, Avenue Road and Rocky Lane. On its last stage of its short length, the brook flows parallel with Cheston Road, heads over Thimblemill Lane and Holborn Hill in Nechells and goes along with Long Acre to Cuckoo Bridge. Soon after, it joins the River Tame at Salford, by Spaghetti Junction.

The first major work on the Hockley Brook was between 1879 and 1880 when it was deepened, widened and brick inverted for the whole of its course from Thimblemill Lane to Hockley. This was a stretch of two and a third miles and it involved the rebuilding or widening of twelve bridges, the diversion of the course of the brook in some places and the carrying of the brook via a double iron syphon under the Fazeley Canal in Nechells.

This work was difficult and expensive at a sum of £20,000, but it was thought that the result would be the prevention of flooding and 'the great benefit of health and cleanliness to the district'. However, these improvements meant that when rain was heavy, there was a quicker delivery of water to the lower part of the stream that resulted in more flooding. So between 1885 and 1895, more work was carried out on the brook in Aston and Nechells. Then at the turn of the twentieth century, the Hockley Brook was diverted and improved near to the border between Winson Green and Smethwick.

Clearing up after the flooding of the Hockley Brook.

A view from Boulton Road, Handsworth of the Hockley Brook flowing freely in April 1928. Notice the Romany vardo, caravan, on the right. Of course, the nearby Black Patch Park had been the main gathering point of local Romanies until they were thrown off by the authorities in the early twentieth century.

Unfortunately, problems continued and during bad storms, the Hockley valley was always the part of Birmingham that was affected the worst by flooding. The realisation of this fact led to the Hockley Brook Scheme. Completed between 1917 and 1929, it cost the huge sum of £758,000 and was of the largest projects of its kind in Britain. Because of its size, the scheme was carried out in sections and began downstream. So the flooding of 1923 occurred because the Hunters Vale and Villa Street localities had not yet benefited from the improvements.

The scheme involved a general lowering and regrading of the bed of the brook and widening where necessary. It was dangerous work and the authorities emphasised that extreme caution was needed 'owing to the ever present risk of floods'. To protect the workers in long culverts, special precautions were taken such as the provision of electric alarms and exit shafts. Overall, this scheme was a success, although more work on the Hockley Brook took place in the early 1950s.

The Day Roy Rogers Came

They were bostin those Cowboy films we used to watch on a Saturday at the local picture house. You'd sit there engrossed by the action, but in your mind you weren't in the Kingsway, the Rock, the ABC or wherever. No, you were there in the Wild West, riding your horse as the trusted sidekick of the hero, the man from whom all baddies fled, the man who ensured that good always triumphed and that wrong was always punished.

Living the film as you did, you were so wound up that when it was over and you came rushing out into the daylight you couldn't wait to play Cowboys with your mates. Can you recall how you quickly shaded your eyes with a salute of your hand and then so soon as you'd got used to the brightness you were off. You'd slap your left thigh with your left hand, because of course the lower half of your body was the horse, and your right hand was your gun. That was made by bringing your thumb down to hold your fourth and little fingers against your palm, whilst your second and index fingers were thrust outwards to make the barrel.

Then you'd run down the horse road, crying out 'Giddyup! and making exploding noises with your mouth, as if you really were the Lone Ranger or Roy Rogers or Buck Jones or Hop Along Cassidy and it was you riding the range chasing the baddies and saving the day.

And what a thrill it was when one year Father Christmas brought you a cap gun from Woolies and a cowboy hat and waistcoat! You really were able to dream that you were a famous lawman as you called out 'Hi Ho Silver!' and joined in the posse (of your mates of course) to track down the villain and bring him to justice. But even that thrill was overwhelmed by the excitement of actually seeing Roy Rogers, as hundreds upon hundreds of kids did back in 1954 when he came to Brum with Trigger.

He sold out for several nights at the Hippodrome and even fetched Trigger on to the stage. What must he have made of all those Brummie kids whooping and hollering and shooting their cap guns or their wooden pistols made by their dads can only be imagined. But it must have been a great day, the day Roy Rogers came to Brum.

Excited grown ups feeding Trigger on 1 March 1954. Thanks to the Birmingham Evening Mail.

Trigger was stabled at Mitchell's and Butler's but Jessie Stauland, nee Harrington, remembers that he was also stabled in town. She writes that 'from the time I was 18 months old I lived in the Corporation Yard in Holliday Street, my Dad worked there. Well I can also recall Roy Rogers and Trigger coming to Brum, because all the horses that were used to sweep the roads were stabled there. Because there were lots of stables therefore Trigger stayed there too.

'I can recall the local children waiting by the gates to get a glimpse of him, which was really exciting. Changing the subject I can also remember when we had snow, the horses had their feet covered with Hessian - to stop them slipping on the sets that were in the Bull Ring, also as soon as there was a snow warning, my Dad and other men used to call for men to come and sweep and clear the snow, there used to be crowds of them, mostly Irish men, so it was very busy where we lived, and fun. They were happy days. I have many happy memories of my school days at St Thomas' School, in Bath and shopping in Broad Street etc. My parents lived there until my Dad retired when he was 65 years old. Then moved to Frankley, which was a big change.'

Eileen Hardwick (nee Bennett) of Bromsgrove is now in her eighties and remembers that 'Roy Rogers had a competition for people to give his horse a name. My brother Alfred Bennett was 14 years old at that time and we lived in Deakins Road, Hay Mills and it was he that named the horse "Trigger" and won the competition and Roy Rogers sent him a signed photo of himself and Trigger, but unfortunately it got lost when we moved house. Unfortunately I lost my brother 5 years ago.'

Roy Rogers visited Carlson House School in Harborne with his wife, Dale Evans, when he made his visit to Birmingham. Janet Chamberlain tells me that 'the school was the first one in Great Britain for Cerebral Palsy Children. Unfortunately I had left the school in 1952 so missed seeing Roy Rogers.'

John Hall saw Roy Rogers when he played the Hippodrome and 'I have the program. He arrived in late February 1954, after travelling over 300 miles from Edinburgh. He and Dale Evans were so popular extra police were on duty to control the crowds. Their show opened on Monday, March 1st, 1954 for a week. They did two shows a day and three on Wednesday and Saturday. Now a lot of people over the years have argued with me that Roy Rogers brought The Sons of the Pioneers with him - he didn't, it was the Whippowills.

'Here's how the show went: 1st, the Hippodrome Orchestra; 2nd, Rags to Riches by Roy and Ronjy; 3rd, Introducing the King of the Cowboys, Roy Rogers and his famous horse Trigger; 4th, Jo, Jac and Joni - Three Goofy Guys; 5th, Roy Rogers introduces The Queen of the West Dale Evans; 6th, The Motons - aerial thrills then intermission; 7th, Roy and Ronjy again; 8th, The Whippowills, and bringing to you again Roy Rogers and Dale Evans; 9th, Waltham and Dorraine and Rolling on Fun; 10th, Roy and Trigger; 11th, Teddie Randall is A Fool among Friends; 12th, Home on the Range with Roy, Dale and the Whippowills.

'It was a great show, Roy did sharp shooting, Trigger did High School tricks. Roy Rogers had a pleasant personality and seemed a very nice man. I was also lucky enough to see Tom Mix when he came here in 1939 and Gene Autry in 1938.'

Sophie-Martin Canning has sent in this cracking photo of her Mom, Carmel 'with her two brothers (lots more came later, but in the early 50s there were just the three!) Pictured are Carmel, Tommy and Johnnie O'Malley. Their grandmother, Nena had taken them in the 50s in their cowboy/girl outfits to see Roy Rogers and Dale Evans at the Aston Hippodrome. My mom, Carmel, was picked from the audience to sit on Trigger!'

Chapel of Ease: Saint Margaret's Ward End

In the Middle Ages it was the law that folk had to worship at their parish church on a Sunday – and that was a tough demand when some parishes were big areas in which many folk lived a good distance away from the place of worship. Aston Parish was one of them. For hundreds of years it included what is now Ashted, Bordesley, Bordesley Green, Deritend, Duddeston, much of Gosta Green, Highgate, Little Bromwich, Nechells, Saltley, Ward End, Washwood Heath and Vauxhall.

The wide extent of Aston meant that it was a long trip for lots of parishioners to reach the parish church of Saint Peter's and Saint Paul's in the old Aston Village, which lay close to the modern Villa Park. The journey was made more difficult for the people of the manors of Saltley, Little Bromwich and Ward End because they had to cross the River Rea. As a result by the 1400s they had a bridge put up which allowed them to travel more easily. The route which led to this crossing became known first as Church Road and then as Aston Church Road in 1895.

Still, it was not an straightforward passage, especially when the Rea flooded because of heavy rain. So, in order to make things better for his tenants, Thomas Bond, the lord of the manor of Ward End, came to an agreement with the vicar of Aston. By this the the people of Ward End would have their own chapel at ease, thus named because it was easier to attend for worship, and their own chaplain. He would have all the collections made at the chapel and the income due to Aston Parish Church from Ward End Park and Irish Meadows. In return, Bond – a clothier from Coventry – paid the vicar of Aston 6s 8d (33 pence).

Little is known of the history of Saint Margaret's thereafter, although there is a story that it was used as a stable by Parliamentarian soldiers in the English Civil War. Indeed, there is no evidence that services were actually conducted there between its foundation and 1835. What is known is that in 1730, it was reported that the chapel was in ruins, as it had been for a long time, and it was undergoing repair paid for by a Mr Blackham, an ironmonger of Birmingham. Whether or not the work was completed is unknown, but in 1781 William Hutton, Birmingham's first historian, wrote disparagingly of Saint Margaret's. He stated that:

> The skeleton of this chapel, in the form of a cross, the fashion of the times, is yet standing on the outward mound; its floor is the only religious one I have seen laid with horse-dung; the pulpit is converted into a manger - it formerly furnished husks for the man, but now corn for the horse. Like the first Christian church, it has experienced a double use, a church and a stable; but with this difference, *that* in Bethlehem was a stable advanced into a church; this, on the contrary, is reduced to a stable.

At last in 1833 the local folk took decisive action. An appeal was launched to rebuild the chapel. It was successful. The mother of Princess Victoria, as then she was, sent

£10, as did Queen Adelaide, the wife of King William IV – although the most generous donation came from local man William Marshall, who gave £500.

The new church of Saint Margaret's was dedicated in 1834 and consecrated seven years later. Then in 1870, it was made a parish church in its own right. In the ensuing decades, so great was the growth of population locally that a mission room was licensed for public worship in Blakeland Street and by the mid-1930s, much of the parish had been handed over to new churches: Saint Paul's, Bordesley Green; Saint Mary and Saint John's, Shaw Hill; and Christ Church, Ward End.

Built in the Gothic style and situated on the junction of the aptly-named Saint Margaret's Road and Church Walk, Saint Margaret's was a village church that reached out to an urban population. Sadly, it will no longer be used a place of worship, despite a vigorous campaign to keep it open by parishioners and local folk staunch in their belief that Saint Margaret's still had a vital role to play in the life of the community. Energised by Audrey Ryan, no-one should diminish their efforts.

Leonard Cowley and his wife Rose 'got married at St Margaret's Church, Ward End on August 25th 1945, sixty years ago next August 2005. I have known my wife since she was born on 25th March 1925. My mother took me around to her house, which was two doors away, about two hours after she was born. I was seven. This will be eighty years ago in 2005. She was always around our house doing errands and playing with

my sister. As the years rolled by she still continued to come around to our house; she used to brush me down and see if I was tidy to meet my girlfriend! She was about twelve years old at that time.

'*I was called up to join the forces in June 1939. After my training I went over to France whereupon no one seemed to know what to do. Eventually, after two weeks train rides, we landed up at Marseilles where we embarked on the troopship HMT Ettrick.*

'*After about eight weeks we landed at Bombay, India. The garrison commander gave us a speech and told us to leave the fruit and women alone and that ten shillings would be stopped from our pay for a blanket to be buried in if we got killed or died out there. Anyhow we boarded a train and after eight days or more landed at Sialkot in Punjab, Napier barracks. The battalion was up the North West Frontier where we joined them at Gamati fighting the tribesmen. We then went further towards Afghanistan where we relieved the Warwickshire regiment. We had a tough time of it.*

'*My wife of today, who was fourteen at the time, wrote to me regularly for five years and when I came home I was so excited I asked her to marry me, so we got engaged. But I was not finished yet so after serving five years in India, Burma, and the North West Frontier on two occasions, I was off again to France, Belgium and Germany for another several months. They transferred me from the Worcestershire regiment to the Royal Welsh Fusiliers straight up the front.*

'*Whilst there an officer told me I was not supposed to be out there. Having served five years in the Far East I came under the Phython scheme and should not have been sent there until I'd had six months at home! When I finally reached home, after the war (but still in the Army on a week's leave) I married Rose and we went on to have four children, nine grandchildren and one great grandchild. I was finally demobbed in June 1946 after I'd spent time clearing mines off the beaches of Wales.*

'*I was very upset when I was told St Margaret's Church was closed down. It was such a beautiful church with happy memories for me. Incidentally my first three children were baptised there in 1946, 1948 and 1950.*'

Beryl Jefferson nee Green has sent in this lovely photo of her father Fred Green, a butcher and part-time fireman during the Second World War at a wedding at Saint Margaret's. Fred is on the far right of the photo. Fred himself was married at Saint Margaret's and later gave his daughter away at her wedding at the same church in 1965. Beryl herself

attended Christ Church, Burney Lane in her teens 'but we shared the same vicar with Saint Margaret's, the Reverend Morgan and Reverend Griffiths in my time. I was also Sunday School teacher and a member of the Youth Club and we met in a hall in Sladefield Road.'

Saint Margaret's in 2004. Thanks to Leonard Cowley.

Lilian Butler now lives in Aldridge but has strong and fond memories of Saint Margaret's Church, Ward End going back to 1929 'when I first became involved as a Sunday school teacher and I was also in the church choir, the services were held in the church rooms in Sladefield Road, I remember Mr. Giles the choir master well. Often we used to hold bazaars in the hall to help raise funds to build Christ Church in Burney Lane, which I believe was opened in 1936/37. I worked at Fort Dunlop and I was able to purchase goods (hot water bottles and aprons) at cost which I donated and sold at a profit. My friend and I used to sit for ages at home making little black cats out of felt, bits and pieces, small buttons too. We stuck pins on the back and made them into 'lucky' brooches, there was always a rush for them.

'There were many different stalls, cakes for example and there was even a 'fortune teller'. The bazaar ran over a three evening period, Thursday, Friday and Saturday and was held annually. Our stall made a lot of money, we worked really hard but we really enjoyed ourselves especially the friendly rivalry between the 'stall holders' seeing who could raise the most money.

'We held a Harvest Festival on October 5th, 1930 and once whilst we were preparing for the service my cousin rushed in to tell us that the R101 airship had just gone up in flames in France. As a Sunday school teacher I used to help to organise concerts, I taught my children songs and dance routines, I even made the outfits, oh, those were the days. Our annual outing was usually to Sutton Park, we travelled by train from Saltley station. Powell's Pool was our destination, we had races, boat rides and picnics. The weather was always good to us and we had such a lot of fun.

'Later, both my husband Raymond and I were confirmed at St. Margaret's and it is there that we took our vows when we married on June 10th 1939. Later, when our daughter was born it was our obvious choice to have her christened there and our son six years later. Memories of those days make me wonder where all of the years have gone.'

Pride of Brum. Saint Philip's

Birmingham's first historian was a man called William Hutton – and as a 17 year old stripling, he tramped here from Nottingham in 1741. When he reached Handsworth Heath, he came into view of a town which was bursting out of its bounds, which was striding forward confidently into history. Before him lay a clutter of buildings, many of which were belching out dark billows which stained the sky black. He was unable to pick out clearly any individual structure – except one, that is. A single building grabbed his attention. It lay on the highest point of the sandstone ridge which towered over the northern side of the valley of the River Rea. The building was St Philip's, uncrowded with houses, for there were none to the north – New Hall excepted – untarnished with smoke and illuminated by a western sun. 'I was delighted with its appearance,' wrote young Will. 'I thought it then, what I do now, and what others will in the future – the pride of the place.'

St Philip's Church is actually a relative newcomer to Brummagem. For centuries, Brummies who were Church of England had only St Martin's to worship in. But in the late 1600s the town was growing rapidly as its workers gained international renown for their skill in making small metal goods. There was a clear need for a new

THE CATHEDRAL.

A tremendous aerial view of Saint Philip's and its churchyard.

church to cater for the burgeoning population, and so between 1711 and 1725 St Philip's was erected. It was placed on the Horse Close, part of a farm which belonged to Robert Phillips, and the builder was a local man named William Shakespeare. He worked to the plans of architect Thomas Archer, a student of Sir Christopher Wren and someone who was influenced greatly by the Baroque buildings he'd seen in his travels in Italy.

It's for this reason that St Philip's has a distinctive Italian-style tower and dome. These were costly additions, and for them to be finished a gift of £600 from George I was needed! But the tower and dome aren't the only attractive features of the church. Far from it. Inside there are four superb stained-glass windows showing *The Nativity, The Crucifixion, The Ascension,* and *The Last Judgement.* They were made by William Morris to the designs of the world-famous Brummie artist Sir Edward Burne-Jones, who was born in Bennett's Hill and was christened in St Philip's itself. Burne-Jones was a leading figure in the pre-Raphaelite movement and many of his paintings now hang in our Art Gallery.

Since its consecration in 1715, St Philip's has played an important part in the life of Brum, not all of it fully realised these days. For nearly 50 years from 1778, for example, musical performances were held at the church to raise money for The General Hospital, which was then in Hospital Street, Summer Lane. Then in May 1830, the church was the starting point for a massive procession of people who supported the extension of the vote to the working and middle classes.

In 1905 it became a cathedral and Dr Charles Gore was the first of the seven Bishops of Birmingham. On Armistice Day 1918 so great was the number of people who wanted to give thanks for the end of the war that three services of prayer had to be held. As the Second World War's storm-clouds drifted over Europe, plans were made to protect the Cathedral's treasures. After war was declared, the exquisite pre-Raphaelite stained glass windows

Another view of St Philip's.

were removed, cleaned and loaded on lorries to be stored in a Welsh mine. It wasn't until 1946 that they next saw daylight. They were replaced by plain glass, and the organ, meanwhile, was dismantled and found a refuge at Pershore Abbey.

The night of 7 November 1940 proved the wisdom of the removals. An incendiary bomb landed on the Cathedral's nave roof, destroying it almost completely. Corrugated iron was hastily pulled over the gaping holes, remaining in place throughout the war, but worshippers of those days recall just one problem. When it rained, services had to be abandoned because neither congregants nor priests could make themselves heard over the noise of raindrops hitting the temporary roof. The nave's roof was repaired with war damage compensation in 1950, but the metal used was too thin for the job.

Saint Philip's has continued to be a focal point for Brummies at times of national and local concern, a caring heart of a caring city. It was here, for example, that prayers were offered up for the safety of our Brummie world-beating yachtswoman Lisa Clayton when she was beset by storms. When St Philip's first rose up in Birmingham's skyline it was a church set in fields, and it lay well outside the built-up area of the town. The Cathedral itself now stands proudly in the middle of Brum.

Saving Souls. The Salvation Army

Praised from continent to continent as the best governed city in the world, Birmingham was a place where the local authority appeared as a model for others to follow its example. Profits flowed into the coffers of the corporation through Joseph Chamberlain's vision of municipalising the private gas and water companies, whilst gas lamps lit up the city's streets and fresh water was piped into every district. This gas and water socialism stimulated by a capitalist and a Liberal was part of a wide and exciting programme of civic action. The building of back-to-back houses was banned, a magnificent Council House rose up on the high ground above the River Rea as a fitting centre for the municipality, and a Parisian-style boulevard swept away the older properties all the way up from New Street to Bagot Street and the Aston Road.

Aptly named Corporation Street, that stretch of this thoroughfare between New Street and the General Hospital was filled with grand buildings, many of them distinctive in their terracotta, which pulled in middle-class shoppers and office workers. Yet for all its justifiably praised achievements, the Birmingham of the late 1800s was a city in which the poor were increasingly separated from the better off.

A gathering of youngsters outside a Salvation Army Hall in 1928 that was sent in to the Evening Mail years back by Mr J. T. Smith of Hockley.

A Salvation Army Band getting ready for an event in the 1950s.

Len Yates recalls an incident during his National Service in 1947. He and his pal were in the 77th Heavy Artillery Regiment at Larkhill on Salisbury Plane, close to Stonehenge. There was a Salvation Army hut in the camp and one night, hungry and having no money and cigarettes, they asked the young Salvation army lady for slate 'like you did back home, but she didn't know what we meant. We explained what you have to is have the goods you want and pay at the week end. She offered pen and pencil to write to our loved ones and even said she would pay the stamp. We started to feel very guilty until she confided in the Salvation Army major.'

The major told them the lady was a wonderful woman and that they could have what they wanted without signing, trusting the Brummie lads to pay at the weekend. 'We were told later that she had worked all over the world with the troops. I think all the chaps and girls in the forces were her family. To me at that time she gave me a cheese roll and a hot cup of tea, but to thousands of service people during the war years at home and abroad the Salvation Army gave their all.

'I can remember during the Birmingham bombing before the dust had settled they would turn up with their tea wagon and made sure all the families had a place to stay and they fed all the workers and firemen. I would like to say the Sally Ann as it was called are due more praise than they get.'

As the wealthy headed for the clean air and tree-lined roads of Edgbaston, Handsworth and Gravelly Hill, the lower middle class and prosperous of the working class also made their way to newer suburbs – heading to Alum Rock, Sparkhill, Bournbrook, Kings Heath and the outermost edges of Small Heath, Aston and Nechells. Within the old city lay a huge population of poorer Brummies encircling the central business and shopping area. Forgotten by most of the well off, excluded from the running of their city and marginalised by all bar themselves, the poor forged close-knit neighbourhoods. And it was amongst them that the Salvation Army focused its efforts, both religiously and socially.

Founded by William Booth to reach out beyond the established churches to the poor who did not attend church, the Salvation Army was a working-class movement. Its soldiers spoke to the poor in their own language with no condescension and no air of superiority. And its men and women practised what they preached, asking no-one to do anything that they had not done themselves. Founded officially in London in 1878, within two years the Salvation Army had already established its first hall in Bordesley Street, when it purchased a former chapel of Carrs Lane Town Mission.

Geoff Hodges has written in on behalf of his mom and dad, Harry and Jessie Hodges, to tell us about the Salvation Army in Aston. Harry has kindly sent me a number of precious photos and this one shows the Aston Citadel band outside Aston Hall in 1937.

On the top row from the left are W. Scott, F. Mason, Harry Hodges, C. Hetherington, S. Summers, G. Boutwood and Moran. Along the second row are F. Taylor, G. Formby, F. Wright, A. Osborne, H. Yardley, W. Stevenson and L. Osborne. And the front row is made up of E. Billingham, F. Jameson, V. Frankum, H. Reynolds, A. Chamblin, W. Turk, N. Baker, Bandmaster M. Popele, J, Matthews, A. Frankum, F. Chamkin, J. Lamb, D. Mason, F. Broves, G. Yardley and A. Lamb.

Harry's grandfather, Harry Jameson, came from Dublin to live in Frederick Road, Aston and was an early member of the Salvation Army. Harry tells us that the first Salvationists locally were in Legge Street and were led by William Leckonby and wife. The Aston Salvation Army then moved to Victoria Road in 1902. Harry himself 'was the drummer for over 50 years. He was the one that woke people up every Sunday morning with the open air service in Aston streets. Also marching down Lichfield Rd to Aston Cross by the clock for Sunday night Open Air Service.'

Len Osborne who is named on this photo is now in his late nineties years 'and was surprised to see the write up on Aston Salvation Army, sent in by our drummer's grandson Harry Hodges. I am a member of that band, also my brother Albert Osborne. I played for over 30 years in the band, and my brother played on cornet until he was 80. Unfortunately my wife and son were bombed out twice in Aston, while I was away on Active Service (Army). She managed to purchase a small general stores at Walsall, for somewhere to live, so we all transferred to Walsall SA after the war.

'I had a homemade sweet shop opposite St Mary's Church, which did stand on the corner of the main Aston Brook Street, and my son Peter, then 5 years old attended St Mary's Church School. This was also about 1937-8. I used to catch the tram outside my shop at 6am in the morning to town, fare 1 penny (1d) to the fruit market (rag market after) and purchase a skip of Worcester Permain apples for 2/6d about 28 lbs. Back on the tram, another 1d for making apples on a stick, I used to buy the large meat wooden skewers, from my local butcher, which had very sharp points on which went into the apple easy. We did well with school children from St Mary's School at a 1d each.

'Also it seems as though a lot of my past had been brought to mind. I was born in New Town Row, New St, by the Old Globe Cinema 1909, in a one up one down court house, later in life married, and lived at St Stephen's St, New Town, where I was christened.'

In 1881 a second hall was opened in Heaton Street Hockley and by 1892 the Salvation Army boasted nine places of worship in the city. The largest was the Birmingham Citadel in Corporation Street, which drew in 1,000 and more worshippers to its services. The other places of worship were in the heart of working-class Brummagem: George Street, Balsall Heath, Green Lane, Small Heath; Legge Street; and Nursery Road Lozells.

At Bertha Road, Greet the Salvation Army followers gathered in the local barracks, in a loft above a stable – and over the next few years, meeting places were set up at other barracks in Granville Street, Ronald Road, Saltley and Shipway Road, Hay Mills. This was the kind of accommodation which would have been shunned by other churches.

But the Salvation Army men and women did more than worship and seek to convert, they reached out to the poorest and most vulnerable, helping their brothers and sisters with deeds as well as words. It is a way of life followed still by Salvation Army members in Birmingham. They are people who carry out the teachings of Jesus to love thy neighbour as thyself.

Dreams of Speedway. The Brummies

Les Marshall was a dreamer. He dreamed of forming a speedway stadium in Birmingham, of bringing together talented riders who would race for a team that carried the city's name, and pulling in thousands of supporters to cheer on that team. But if Les Marshall had dreams then he was no fantasist. He was prepared to toil and moil to make his dreams come true. He was ready to graft as hard as he could to ensure that speedway would succeed in post-war Birmingham.

It was in the north Birmingham area in 1945 that Les found his site – the bomb damaged Birchfield Harriers Sports ground where Italian prisoners of war were kept in the grandstand. Les was not deterred by the mess it was in. He got cracking as quick as he could, buying disused lamp standards from the council and fetching in ash from the gas works. With his own hands he shovelled the ash in terracing. Making pits from water tanks, he fashioned safety fences from jeep cases and entrances from Anderson Shelters. At last he was ready and in 1946 the first speedway meeting at the new Perry Barr track pulled in 15,000 excited and supportive fans.

Attendances boomed, as they did at all speedway tracks, but things weren't a bed of roses. Joining speedway's first division in 1950, Les lost the huge sum of £10,000 but he and his manager – the Australian speedway veteran Tiger Hart – went on to put together a smashing side. Captained by England's Alan 'Whacker' Hunt, two years

The 1952 Brummies at Perry Barr.

later the team provided three riders amongst the 16 who battled it out for the first prize in the World Championship final at a floodlit Wembley.

The youngest and newest rider was the exhilarating Dan Forstberg from Sweden. Then there was Arthur Payne, an Australian who had enjoyed a really good season and Graham Warren, another Australian. Nicknamed the 'Blond Bombshell', Graham was rated the best rider in the world back in 1950, he had a bad smash that broke his skull

In the late 1940s and 1950s Doreen Chapman and her late husband 'went down to Perry Barr of a Saturday night and had a good night for about 10/-. We used to go on the bus. The tops were red and yellow. We named our first son Graham after Graham Warren.' This photo was taken in the 1950s and shows Graham Warren and 'a young lad, but I don't know who he is. They used to have a lot of cycle speedway at Kingstanding.'

Ken Spurrier also looks back on the late 40's with affection, but 'the one thing that has always been in my mind was the National Trophy of 1948. Brummies had a marvellous team, Stan Dell, captain, Ray Dook, Doug McLachlan, Roy Wilson, Graham Warren and of course Dick Tolly. Brummies lost an 18 head first leg at West Ham 67-41 and there was not much hope for a mere Provincial league team such as us against the mighty London team in the second leg. The Hammers were "hammered" in the second leg. By heat seven the Brummies had wiped out the 26 point deficit and went on to win 85-23. In the glorious sunshine of that beautiful summer the Birmingham team left a memory for me for the last 50 odd years.

'Indeed in the match programme the following week, Les Marshall said: 'In 50 years time, Brummie supporters will talk of old times and someone will say "Do you remember 1948 against West Ham?" Well, Carl, I have and do still remember.'

in three places. Coming back from that, some though he had lost some of his verve and panache – but to his army of Brummie fans, Graham Warren was a thrilling rider. A Brummie victory was not to be, although Dan Forsberg rode spectacularly, winning two heats and then dropping out of contention after he fell in his last ride. And the Brummies were runners-up in the national league. Unhappily, speedway nationally had begun a rapid decline and the Brummies closed down in 1957.

A speedway revival from the late 1960s saw the Brummies emerge again in 1971. Twelve years later, the club left Perry Barr due to redevelopment and after two seasons at Bordesley Green it closed in 1986. Speedway fans still call for the rebirth of the Brummies and for the chance to cheer on men like Alan Hunt and Graham Warren.

I would like to thank Betty Melley for help in this article.

Dot Goode, her husband and friends used to go every week to watch the Brummies 'and also to some of their away matches'. This photo was taken in Ventor Road, Hockley 'when we were going to Belle Vue with them. How we loved Stan Dell, Charlie Appleby, Tiger Hart, Graham Warren and a few I can't remember by name. How we enjoyed ourselves but how dirty we always went home, but who cared. We had some fun. Les Marshall was a very nice man. They were wonderful days.

Barbara Hart contacted me about her famed father, 'Tiger' Hart. She tells me that he 'was in fact born in Balham, London in 1907, not Australia. He did sail to Australia in 1924 on the RMS Ormonde en-route for Brisbane where he farmed in various parts of the outback, not too successfully. He then met up with the great Frank Arthur, and under his guidance started racing on local circuits (Australia being the birth of speedway). Frank advised him to return to England which he did in 1930. Birmingham Speedway was first located at Hall Green. I have a treasured programme dated June 8, 1938, when my father first captained the team. My brother John rode there with Arthur Browning and co. The team won many accolades.'

Phil 'Tiger' Hart is recalled well by Vic Secker, who first suggested to me that I write about the Brummies. Thanks Vic, who is of the firm opinion that the best 'years were 1946 and 1947, when I believe that Phil 'Tiger' Hart was team captain and Stan Dell was vice captain. I also remember Charlie and Ernie Appleby, same name but not related, to my knowledge. What lingers most in my memory is of standing on one of the bends and being sprayed with cinders as the four riders jostled for position, and no-one in the crowd minded getting dirty. The outstanding thing was the bonhomie that existed between home fans and the opposing fans alike. No fighting or arguing at all if your team lost or won. What a pity such geniality does not exist among fans of other sports today as it did then.'